EXAM *Revision* NOTES

AS/A-LEVEL
ICT

Ian Ⓟaget

Philip Allan Updates, an imprint of Hodder Education, part of Hachette Livre UK, Market Place, Deddington, Oxfordshire OX15 0SE

Orders
Bookpoint Ltd, 130 Milton Park, Abingdon, Oxfordshire OX14 4SB
tel: 01235 827720
fax: 01235 400454
e-mail: uk.orders@bookpoint.co.uk

Lines are open 9.00 a.m.–5.00 p.m., Monday to Saturday, with a 24-hour message answering service. You can also order through the Philip Allan Updates website: www.philipallan.co.uk

© Philip Allan Updates 2008
ISBN 978-0-340-95951-0

First printed 2008
Impression number 5 4 3 2 1
Year 2013 2012 2011 2010 2009 2008

Printed in Spain

Hachette Livre UK's policy is to use papers that are natural, renewable and recyclable products and made from wood grown in sustainable forests. The logging and manufacturing processes are expected to conform to the environmental regulations of the country of origin.

Contents

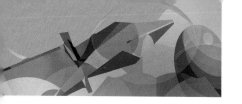

Introduction

1 Using this book

You can use this book to revise for AS- and A-level Information and Communications Technology (ICT) for any of the main examination boards (OCR, WJEC, AQA) as it covers topics which are found in all the specifications, many of them common to all three.

It should be noted, however, that this is a *revision* book. It does not attempt to delve deeply into any of the topics covered. You should study individual sections using other available textbooks, your lesson notes and attending classes etc. This book is to be used *after* you have studied the subject.

The book is divided into 13 topics. Roughly, Topics 1 to 7 cover work done in AS and Topics 8 to 13 cover the A2 work. However, because of the overlap in some specifications, you should check the headings indicated on the contents page against the topics you need.

Use this book to:
- remind yourself of the essential vocabulary
- find topic summaries
- revise the advantages and disadvantages of various ICT systems and practices

It also be can used successfully alongside the AS and A2 *ICT Student Workbooks*, published by Philip Allan Updates.

2 Revision

Revision is an *active* undertaking. You cannot revise successfully using reading skills alone. There are a number of ways of making sure that what you are revising stays in your long-term memory.
1 After you have read a section, put the book down and summarise the essential points in writing.
2 Get hold of past examination questions and answer them. Always check the kind of answers the examiners are looking for by looking at the published mark scheme.
3 Revise with a friend or get a family member to test you.
4 Revise at a desk or table, not lying in bed.

3 Examination technique

The first and foremost technique is to *be prepared*. The examination is a test of what you have learned in the past year or 2 years and your head will not magically fill with answers on the day of the exam. If you are properly prepared you will relax more easily.

Be fully aware of the nature of the exam paper before you go into the exam room. You should complete several mock papers and have a good idea of the format of the examination, how many questions to expect, whether there are any choices and so on.

In all questions, it is important to look out for the signs for what the examiner requires, such as the following **key words**:

- Give…
- State…
- Identify…
- Describe…
- Explain…
- Compare…
- Contrast…
- Discuss…

Take note also of the number of lines to be filled in and the number of marks to be awarded.

Once you have answered a question, read through your answer and try to see where the examiner could have given you marks. Have you done enough? Remember that repeating a certain point in different words does not work in ICT. You have to gain each mark with something new.

Briefly, the key words will require the following responses (but keep your wits about you as there are no hard and fast rules here):

- **Give**, **state**, or **identify** requires a word, phrase or sentence and will usually be worth 1 mark.
- **Describe** requires at least a sentence. (Look at the marks available to know how many points to make.)
- **Compare** or **contrast** mean that you need to identify a factor common to two systems and describe that factor for each.
- **Explain** probably requires a description of how or why something is done and perhaps an advantage or disadvantage or some other factor described.
- **Discuss** is the highest order of question. You need to cover the advantages and disadvantages of something, make points and expand them and finally reach a conclusion.

The examiners may use other key words, but they will probably have similar meanings to the above. The main thing to be aware of when answering questions is: 'What is the examiner trying to get me to write? Which part of the specification is being examined?'

Finally, if you finish early, don't doodle on the front of the examination paper. That gives the wrong impression to an examiner. Go over your questions and check that where there are, say, 4 marks, you have given an answer where the examiner can put four ticks. If it is a discussion question, check that you have explained yourself well.

Units used in ICT

All units in ICT are based around the **binary system**. This is sometimes called the **base two** number system because there are only two digits in it – 0 and 1 – and all data is made up of combinations of 0 and 1.

These are the units of storage:

- 1 **bit** is a 0 or a 1.
- 1 **byte** is 8 bits.
- 1 **Kilobyte** (1K) is 1024 bytes.
- 1 **Megabyte** (1MByte) is 1024 Kilobytes.
- 1 **Gigabyte** (GByte) is 1024 Megabytes.

A bit can hold a 0 or a 1. It can be used to represent two-state concepts such as TRUE or FALSE, MALE or FEMALE, YES or NO.

A byte can hold a character, such as the letter A or the character 7 or the symbol ?.

A Kilobyte can hold 1024 characters or approximately one page of this book.

A Megabyte is about the size of a digital photo.

A Gigabyte can hold approximately 1 billion characters.

Speed of transmission of data is measured by how fast 1 bit can travel in 1 second. This is know as a **baud**. The speed is called the **baud rate**. Sometimes speed of transmission (line speed) is measured in bits per second (bps), in kbps if the speed is 1024 times faster, or in mbps if it is over a million times faster (where the k stands for kilo and m for mega).

The capacity of a communications channel is known as its **bandwidth**, and measures the range of frequencies a channel can handle. Bandwidth is measured in **hertz (Hz)**. Channels with a large bandwidth are known as **broadband**, usually many KHz or MHz, whereas bandwidths lower than around 3KHz are called **narrow band**.

Finally…

Working with a revision text is an active task. It's not just about reading, but about remembering and associating facts learned in this book with those learned elsewhere. Definitions and descriptions, advantages and disadvantages have to be learned, just as you may have to learn a poem, the dialogue of a play or a piece of music for other subjects. In addition to learning facts, you need to understand that these facts can be fitted to different scenarios. Revising can be hard work, but in the end very rewarding. If you can go into the examination room, open your paper and see ICT terms with which you are familiar and questions you can answer with confidence, you will feel well rewarded for your efforts.

Good luck with your revision and your examinations. I hope you find this book useful. Remember what the polar explorer drank — ICT!

1 Data

There are many other characters, such as foreign characters.

Data forms the raw materials given to a process as inputs. It may take many forms, e.g. digits, letters, other characters such as $, ?, +, or anything else that could be stored in a computer system.

Data is meaningless unless it is given a **context** or an **interpretation**. For instance, 110991 could represent a number, but given the context of 'date of birth' it becomes 11 September 1991.

It is the same with the way data is held in the computer. Everything held in the computer is changed to millions of 0s and 1s. If you were able to turn the random access memory (RAM) of a computer into numbers (known as **binary digits**), it would look something like 01000111010101010101010101... and so on for millions of digits. In order to know what the binary data means it must be interpreted.

You will know, for instance, from your work on databases, that different data types have to be defined as text, number, currency etc. This is so that the computer program can interpret the binary data as a number, a letter, a picture or whatever.

1.1 Information

DATA + INTERPRETATION = INFORMATION

Once we know how to interpret the data, we then have some **information**.

Complex interpretation is sometimes needed to gain information from data. We may need **context**, **structure** and **meaning** to get our information.

In the date example above, the data is 110991. If we are aware that this data is in the context of a date in England, then our awareness of the structure of 'dates' helps us to interpret the first two digits as days, the second two as the month and the third two as the year. If the data represented a date in the USA, a different known structure would lead us to interpret the same data to give the meaning 9 November 1991. If someone gave us the data 110991 and told us that this was a date in November, then our knowledge would help us deduce that this person came from the USA.

1.2 Conveying data

There are many different ways in which data is conveyed or prepared for human use (see Table 1.1).

Method	Use	Where appropriate	Advantage	Disadvantage
Text	A method of conveying meaning using characters	For writing letters, business reports, computer manuals	It is possible to convey detailed meaning using text. Instructions can be given	Unless you know the code or language used you cannot understand it
Picture	A visual representation of an object	In an advertisement for selling a house	The customer can see immediately what the house looks like without having to read a description	The image may be misleading if cropped or doctored in some way
Video	Conveying a moving image	For showing an event, such as a football game	Conveys a realistic image of what happens over time	Because it is made of a number of pictures, a vital piece of data may be missed between frames
Animation	Creation of apparent movement on the computer screen	For showing that the CPU is occupied, e.g. with an hour-glass animation	Instantly understandable if the symbols used are known	You may not know the meaning of the animation, therefore it will convey no meaning
Sound	To draw your attention to something by means of a sound	When an error has been made; when a new message arrives; when a fire is detected	You are made aware that the event has occurred even if you are not watching at the time	If your speakers are switched off you will not hear it. You may be audio-impaired
LED	To draw your attention to an event by use of a light	When the caps lock key is pressed on your computer keyboard	You can see at a glance that the event has occurred	You may not be aware of the colour code for the lights

Table 1.1 Methods of conveying data

1.3 Information and knowledge

Knowledge is the way that we can understand and use the information that we have.

Data given a meaning and context can become information. Information given understanding can be knowledge.

Figure 1.1 shows the data as 2, 3. The information is that the score in a football game was 2 goals for and 3 goals against. Knowledge of the way these things are written tells us that the home team lost.

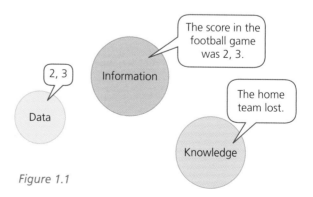

Figure 1.1

1.4 Types of data

Inside the computer or on the storage media, data is held in a never-ending stream of 0s and 1s known as binary numbers. This data is accessed by looking at small sections of it called **words**. In order to interpret the words we must know what the binary numbers represent.

The data was originally stored using a **data type**. This gives the clue to interpreting the data. There are several types, and different packages often use slightly different names to describe them. Some data types are shown below.

Boolean

This data type is known as two-state. It is used when you are describing something that is:

- True or False
- Yes or No
- Male or Female
- On or Off

Character

A character is a single item of data, usually a letter, number or punctuation mark found on the keyboard of a computer, though there are other 'invisible' characters such as *escape* and *line feed/return* which you can press but not see. Examples of characters are:

- 1
- G
- %
- Z
- space

Real

These are numbers which are not whole numbers. This data type is used for storing numbers such as:

- 3.14
- 1.00
- 0.034
- the average score of the class in a test
- the frequency of a radio channel

Integer

An integer is a whole number. This has no fractional part and would be used when counting something such as:

- the number of rooms in a house
- the number of paces walked
- the number of students in a school

In some systems there is no distinction between real and integer and the data type is just called 'number'.

Note that telephone numbers and room numbers are character types.

String

This is a row or 'string' of characters. They do not need to make sense, and are just stored as one unit in the computer. They might be a word, a sentence or a jumble. Examples are:

- cat
- computer
- 12345
- GL19 4XX
- < s;*7!HH

Date/time

Dates and times are complicated, as they hold more than one item of data. For instance, we all know that we can interpret 220307 as 22 March 2007 (if we live in the UK). The 220307 is made up of three separate numbers, each subject to different constraints, such as the number of days in a month. Time is similar as it contains hours, minutes and seconds. This means that dates and times need their own data type. Examples are:

- 18/05/08
- 2:25
- 12:34:57

Static data

Data can be either static or dynamic.

Static data will not change under normal circumstances, such as your name, an airline flight number or the name of your school.

Static data may be stored on read-only media such as a CD or DVD, as it has no need to change very often.

Dynamic data

This type of data may change at any time. Examples include the arrival time of a flight displayed at an airport, the balance of money left in your bank or the information provided by a website offering holidays.

Dynamic data may be stored on hard drives. The World Wide Web contains dynamic data.

Flight XYZ 23 (static data) may be delayed by 50 minutes and land at 12:50 (dynamic data).

1.5 Sources of data

Data is only valuable if it is *accurate* and *reliable*. We must always be careful that data being used is from a trusted source.

Direct and indirect sources

Data may come from a **direct source** or from an **indirect source**.

For instance, a speech given by a politician and then quoted in a newspaper is an example of the use of an indirect source – the newspaper is the 'middle man' (see Figure 1.2).

If you were present at the speech yourself then you would have heard it from the original source.

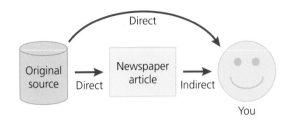

Figure 1.2

Sometimes data can be obtained as a result of processing other data. For example, a computer can produce figures of the most popular holiday destinations of a travel firm by analysing the original data supplied by customers booking the holidays.

Table 1.2 shows some advantages and disadvantages of the two sources of data.

	Advantages	**Disadvantages**
Direct source	• The data is most likely to be accurate and reliable. • The data is most likely to be up to date.	• It can be difficult or embarrassing to ask someone their religion or their annual income, for example. It may be impossible/impractical to collect direct data, for example for an A-level student to conduct a survey on the whole UK population.
Indirect source	• The data is not contaminated by the act of collecting it. For instance, a person may not tell the truth when asked directly about his/her income. • Indirect data may have been collected for a different reason and so will not be biased for the current use. • Reliable indirect sources can provide extensive and verified data when conducting a survey on a large population.	• The data may have changed because of inaccuracies in copying or bias on behalf of the person using them. • The source may not contain all the necessary data. • The data may be out of date.

Table 1.2 Advantages and disadvantages of using direct or indirect data sources

2 Quality of information

Information may not always be correct or true. If you ask someone what his/her birthday is you have no idea whether the reply is correct. You have information, but is it useful or meaningful? Similarly, if you look for information on the internet you must always be prepared to check what you find, as anyone can put anything on a web page and claim it is true.

In business, it is very important to know the quality of information used as it can affect your profits.

Several factors can affect the quality of the information produced:
- accuracy
- relevance
- age
- completeness
- presentation
- level of detail

Factor	Definition	Example
Accuracy	The data needs to be accurate. A name needs to be spelled correctly. A figure needs to have the appropriate number of decimal places.	If an address is stored as 111 Green Street when it is really 11 Green Street, a person's post may not arrive. If a year of birth is wrongly recorded a person may not be offered a pension.
Relevance	The data must be useful for the job being undertaken. It is a waste of storage space to collect data that is not relevant and can slow down searches and other processes when it is in use.	It is not useful to record the number of rooms in a house if you are only interested in posting a letter. It is not usually necessary to ask for gender as well as name, candidate number and centre number on an examination paper.
Age	Data often changes as time passes. The information provided may become out of date.	If you want to know the number of students taking A-level ICT, so you could print the correct number of examination papers, it would not help to have figures that are 5 years old.
Completeness	Incomplete data will usually lead to worthless information.	If you book a holiday and you receive the data of flight number, time and date of departure but not the airport you are to fly from it will be useless.
Presentation	Data must be presented in a sensible way or the information being provided will be difficult to interpret.	Data is often turned into information by using a structure, such as a graph, chart or table. A train timetable is a good example of data presented in a coherent way so as to convey information.
Level of detail	The amount of information provided must be decided carefully. Too much will detract from the understanding of what is being conveyed. Too little and full understanding cannot be achieved.	A railway timetable that also contains the distances between stations and the number of waiting rooms on each platform might be interesting, but could distract the user from finding the time of departure of his/her train.

Table 1.3 Factors affecting the quality of information

3   *Encoding data*

In order to store data it is often advantageous to encode it. If, for example, you are selling three different colours of laptop bags, you might store them as B, W and R rather than writing black, white and red.

There are advantages and disadvantages to storing data in this way.

Advantages of encoding data:
● It takes up less memory space in the computer.
● It is faster to enter the data once you know the codes.
● There should be fewer errors in the accuracy of the data recorded as the input is limited to a certain number of codes or a certain format.

Disadvantages of encoding data:
● People may be confused over a code. For instance, B may mean black but it might equally mean blue or brown.
● By encoding the data you may make it less accurate. B might be for blue but it is not possible to tell if the object is light blue, dark blue, navy blue and so on.
● The person entering the code has to make a judgment. One person's idea of dark grey might be another person's idea of black.
● It is possible to run out of codes. Using single letters of the alphabet means that you can only have 26 colours – which is not useful if you are producing tins of paint.

Remember that nothing will ensure the data being entered is correct, but we *can* make sure that each item has been entered correctly and that it is sensible. For this we use verification and validation.

4 | *Verification and validation*

When data is entered into the computer it needs to be checked. If you type in the wrong thing you will get back rubbish. If the input is wrong, the output will be meaningless. You have probably seen the following acronym:

Figure 1.3

There is no way to tell if an item of data being entered into the computer is correct. If someone writes his/her name on an order form as Mickey Mouse, that is what must be entered into the computer, correct or not. There is no way of telling if Mickey Mouse is really that person's name. However, it is possible to check if each data item has been entered correctly and if it is sensible.

To ensure that data has been entered correctly it is **verified**. The process is known as **verification**. To ensure that data is sensible it can be **validated** – the process for this is known as **validation**.

One way of remembering that verification is done by a human and validation is done by a computer is to remember the word verify as V E R I F 👁 .

4.1 Verification

When you change your password on a computer you are asked to type it a second time to check that you have entered it correctly. In other words, your entry has been verified. This is also known as **double entry with automatic comparison**.

In business, for instance, a firm may place an advertisement in a newspaper for a product it is selling and include an order form along with the advert. When these forms are sent to the firm the data on them has to be entered into the computer. The data is copied from the forms by one operator, then passed to a second operator who keys them in again. If the computer notices a difference between the first data set entered and that entered by the second operator, a warning is issued and the second operator has to check the data being entered more carefully. He/she must decide whether they or the first operator made the mistake and then correct it. If the operator cannot decide, for instance if the writing is unclear, he/she will pass the document to a supervisor to make the decision.

If there is only one operator, for instance when you are filling in an online order form on the computer, you can verify the data by **proofreading**. This means that after you have entered the data you read it through again carefully to make sure that you have not made any mistakes. Another method for a single operator to use is **visual checking**. This is where the operator reads through the data entered, carefully comparing it by eye to the original source.

4.2 Validation

There are a number of ways that data can be checked to see if it is sensible. Some of them are shown below.

Range check
The data entered must be in a sensible range. For instance, if a test is out of 100 marks then only marks in the range 0–100 are acceptable.

Type check
This check ensures that the data type is correct. For instance, if the number of rooms in a house is being recorded it is sensible for this to be an integer, so only integers will be accepted by the database.

Length check
The length of the input is checked. For instance, if a name is being entered into the computer it is reasonable to assume that it will be between 2 and 18 characters long.

Lookup
If the data entered consists of a limited number of possible entries then the computer can compare the entry with a list of allowed answers. For instance, if the predicted grade for your examination can be A, B, C, D, E or U then only these inputs will be allowed.

Remember that verification *cannot* ensure the data is correct.

Remember that these validation methods can only ensure that reasonable or sensible data is input to a system. There is no certainty that the data is accurate or true.

Picture or format check

The data being entered has a particular pattern, such as a post code or a car registration number. The computer checks to see that the entry conforms to that pattern.

Presence check

Some of the data being entered must be present. For instance, if you are ordering goods on the internet you have to give your address and the item you are ordering. An error will occur if this data is not filled in and the computer will not allow the processing to take place.

Integrity check

Sometimes it is possible to check the data by comparing it with something else known to the system. For instance, if the data is a form to enter a particular race for a certain age group and the system knows the date of birth of the individual, it can cross check to see that the user is allowed to enter that race.

Check digit

A check digit only validates data implicitly. It is a useful aid to verification. For example, the new International Standard Book Numbers (ISBNs) have 13 digits. The thirteenth digit is the check digit. When the book number is assigned, a computer works out the thirteenth digit using an algorithm. This same algorithm is run on the first 12 digits when the ISBN is entered by a user. If the check digit produced by that algorithm is the same as the entered check digit then the input is deemed to be valid.

5   *Test data*

When systems are created it is important to check that they are working satisfactorily – that they produce the results they are supposed to produce. The system could be, for example, a computer program, a database or a spreadsheet model.

First the system would need testing by the programmer of the system. This is known as **white box testing** or **alpha testing**. This is usually carried out as the program is being developed. Each individual part of the system will be carefully tested to make sure that formulae, loops and links work properly and that the system produces the correct results for a given set of inputs.

The developer will work to a **test plan** which was set up when the system was being designed. The test plan would give:
- the part of the system to be tested
- the data it would be tested with
- the expected outcome of that test

Systems are often tested with data that is:
- normal data – data that would be expected to be input
- extreme data – on the edges of the range of data that could be expected
- erroneous – data that is definitely wrong, such as a date of birth being entered into a telephone number field

There are many high-profile cases where badly tested systems caused chaos or even death. Try to find out about some of them.

When the producers of the system feel that it can be tested by the users, samples of the system are distributed to be tested 'in the field'. This is known as **black box testing** or **beta testing**. Here, the system is put into use to see how it copes with being used by people who have no knowledge of how the system was built. They only see the surface of the system – the processes inside are invisible – hence the idea of the black box: you cannot see into it.

6 *Backup and archive*

When you are working with computers many things can go wrong, each of which can cause you to lose or damage your data. Some causes are:
- electrical disturbance, such as that caused by thunderstorms
- power cuts, or even someone switching off your power supply when you did not expect it
- machine failure, such as a disc crash
- human error (the most common cause), for example where you save using the same name as an existing file or delete something without thinking

This loss of data can be extremely annoying, and in business can have serious consequences. For instance, you may lose an address book with all your business contacts in it. The answer is to make sure that the data you are currently working with is **backed up**. This is where live copies of your work are saved on a medium other than the one you are working with. If backups are made every day then the worst that can happen is that 1 day's work is lost.

After a period of time, data that you have saved is no longer relevant, for instance a record of last year's sales. However, for various reasons you may wish to retain this data permanently and so it can be **archived**. This means data is stored on a CD or DVD and then removed from the hard drive of your computer. If you ever need that data back again it can be retrieved from the archive.

7 *Cost of information*

Information is valuable. Many firms go to great lengths and spend a huge amount of money to gather data about their customers, in order to gain information about their spending habits which allows them to alter their production accordingly. Loyalty cards are one way in which this information can be gathered. However, there are costs involved in collecting this valuable data and in producing information from it.

The costs are incurred by the following:
- The hardware needed to collect, hold and process the data has to be purchased initially and then kept, maintained and renewed as necessary.
- The software has to be purchased and upgraded as necessary.
- The consumables, such as paper, toner and ink cartridges, must be paid for.
- The personnel to work at collecting the data and producing the information must be paid. They need occasional training and will need office space, all of which cost money.

8 *Input–process–output–feedback loop*

In every computer system there has to be an **input**, otherwise there would be no way in which the outcomes could ever change.

There has to be a **process** in order for the system to process the data input and produce an output.

There has to be an **output** if the results of what have been processed are ever to be known.

Additionally, it is sometimes necessary to **store** results for later use, and it is important to store the computer programs that are managing the computer system.

As a result of the output of the system, there may be **feedback** to enable the system to react to this new information.

The whole system is shown in Figure 1.4.

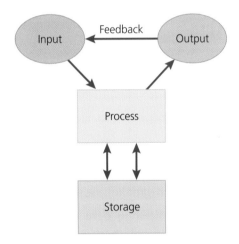

Figure 1.4 The input–process–output–feedback loop

8.1 Examples of the input–process–output–feedback loop

A fire alarm

Input	Smoke is detected, message sent to processing
Process	Concludes a fire is taking place, sends message to alarm system (the output)
Output	Bell begins to ring, message sent to fire station
Feedback	Smoke is as a result of burnt toast
Input	Reset the alarm
Process	Send signal to output
Output	Bell stops ringing

Booking a holiday

Input	John uses his computer to book a holiday online
Process	The system takes John's details and processes them
Output	Message sent to John to say holiday is booked
Feedback	The system is given the information that the holiday is no longer available
Input	Jane uses her computer to book the same holiday online
Process	The system takes Jane's details and processes them
Output	Message sent to Jane advising her that the holiday is no longer available and suggesting another

Topic summary

Data/information — data with context, structure and meaning gives information.

Methods of conveying data — text, picture, video, animation, sound, LED.

Information/knowledge — data + interpretation = information; information + understanding = knowledge.

Types of data — Boolean, character, real, integer, string, date/time, static, dynamic.

Sources of data — direct or indirect.

Quality of data — affected by accuracy, relevance, age, completeness, presentation, level of detail.

Encoding data — useful for storing data; has advantages and disadvantages.

Verifing data — can be done by double entry, proofreading or visual check.

Validating data — can be done by different types of check: range, type, length, lookup, picture or format, presence, integrity, check digit.

Test data — white box or alpha testing; test plan using normal, extreme and erroneous data; black box or beta testing.

Backup and archive — backing up to avoid loss of data; archiving to store data.

Cost of information — costs of hardware, software, consumables, personnel required to collect information.

Input-process-output-feedback loop — the information handling stages in a computer system.

TOPIC 2 — Software and hardware components

Note the spelling of software and hardware.

1 The difference between hardware and software

Hardware – the physical part of the computer, including the processor, storage, input and output devices.

Software – the programs which make the computer work, such as operating systems and application packages, and the data in the storage of the computer.

2 Input, output and storage devices

These devices are known as peripherals. Remember that the device is the drive. The CD, disc or DVD is the medium that goes into the drive.

Type of device	Description	Examples
Input device	A device for accepting data and submitting it to the processor	Keyboard, microphone, touch screen, mouse, scanner, joystick
Output device	A device which translates the signals from the processor and puts them into a format readable by humans or suitable to be put back into the computer at a later stage	Printer, screen, speaker, lights (LEDs)
Storage device	A device that can store data in an electronic or optical format which can only be read by the computer	Hard drive, USB flash memory, optical disc drives (CD drive, DVD drive)

Table 2.1 Types of devices

3 Specialist hardware and software

3.1 Specialist hardware devices

Many peripheral devices have been developed for special reasons, for instance for people who cannot see, hear or use their hands. Specialist peripheral devices include:

- Braille keypad – input device for the visually impaired
- mouth-stick – input device for someone who cannot use his/her hands
- puff–suck tube – input device for someone who cannot use his/her hands
- eye-typer – input device that uses the muscles around the eye to move a pointer
- foot-mouse – input device controlled by the foot
- embosser – output device that produces raised Braille characters on paper for those who cannot see

3.2 Specialist software

Help can be given by the software:

- Text to speech – changes any text written on the screen into speech. Suitable for people who cannot read what is written on the screen.
- Screen magnifier – text can be enlarged for those who need it, or individual parts of the screen can be enlarged.

4 Types of software

The programs used by the computer are loosely arranged into different types as shown in Table 2.2.

Type of software	Description	Examples
Applications program	A computer program for carrying out a simple task	• A program used for keeping household accounts • A text editing program • A program to design DVD labels
Applications package (generic programs)	Each application contains a set of programs with user documentation which can be used for a variety of tasks within the remit of the application	• A word processor for any word-processing tasks • A spreadsheet program that can be used for a variety of mathematics-based tasks • A database program for storing, querying and reporting data • A desktop publishing program used for many kinds of publishing such as posters, flyers and news-sheets • Presentation software for producing presentation slides, which may include sound and video
Systems software	Programs that control the operation of the computer	• Disc formatter • Network software • Operating systems • Printer spoolers • Drivers • Anti-virus software • Translators

Table 2.2 Types of software

5 User interfaces

A user interface is the way in which humans and computers can communicate with each other. The computer works in binary numbers and the human does not. Different interfaces are suitable for different needs. Often, as in well-known operating systems, more than one user interface is available.

5.1 Graphical user interface (GUI)

A graphical user interface (GUI) replaces words with small self-explanatory pictures known as icons. This allows access to applications using a mouse and a pointer instead of typing in commands. This method is often thought to be

intuitive – it is possible to use without a lot of training. It is the basis of the systems using 'windows', favoured by all the major computer software producers.

Figure 2.1 Graphical user interface with icons

5.2 Command-based interface or command line interface (CLI)

A command-based interface or command line interface (CLI) is one where the commands have to be typed in before the computer responds. Thus, to run a word processor you would have to type a command and press the enter key. The problem with this method is that a user needs to know the commands in advance. It is not intuitive like a GUI. However, an advantage is that more exact commands can be given to the computer than is possible by just clicking icons.

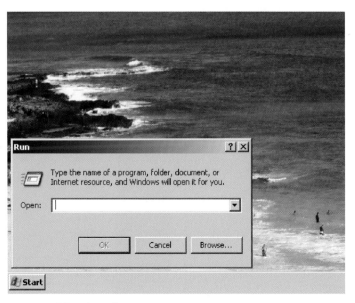

Figure 2.2 Command line interface

5.3 Forms-based interface

A forms-based interface is one in which the user is restricted to an area of the screen called a form, on which a series of spaces is left for the user to fill in. Any online ordering system will probably use this type of interface. It restricts the user to a limited number of responses and makes sure that all the necessary data has been collected before proceeding. It is also the basis of many tasks carried out on the computer. For instance, if a document is to be printed, a form will appear where the user can fill in how many copies, which printer to use etc.

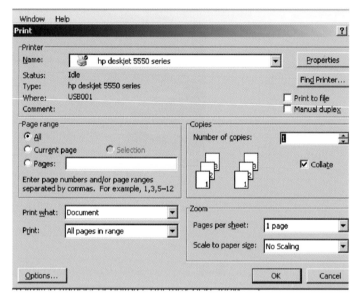

Figure 2.3 Forms-based interface

5.4 Menus

Menus, sometimes called drop-down menus, restrict the user to a limited number of options, but they also show the user all the options available for that particular command. Menus sometimes have **sub-menus**.

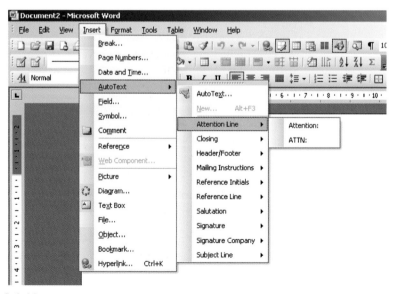

Figure 2.4 Menus

5.5 Natural language interface

A natural language interface is one which utilises the user's own language to communicate with the computer. You could do this by talking to the computer: 'Computer, please print my document.' Alternatively, you could type your commands in words or, on devices such as pocket organisers, use handwriting.

5.6 Windows, icons, menus, pointers (WIMP)

Many of the characteristics of the interfaces mentioned above can be combined to create the windows, icons, menus, pointers (WIMP) interface. The WIMP interface uses a pointer, moved by a mouse, with selections made by clicking the mouse, or another pointing device.

5.7 Advantages and disadvantages of interfaces

GUI (windows)

Advantages

- It is an intuitive approach and easy to use.
- Little or no training is needed.
- Using a mouse makes opening and closing packages quicker than other methods.
- Multiple windows can be open at once.

Disadvantages

- It requires significant system resources in terms of memory and speed of processing.
- Some commands to the operating system may not be possible using the GUI.

CLI

Advantages

- You can type in the exact item you are inquiring about.
- Customers are used to words and know the name of the item they want to find.

Disadvantages

- The system may not accept your spelling of the item.
- It is difficult to explain distinctions to the system, for example the difference between a large or small frying pan.
- It looks old fashioned and may not portray a modern image to the public.

Forms

Advantages

- The user is restricted to certain responses.
- Validation of individual entries is possible.
- Input can be recorded directly to a database.

Disadvantages

- It is not possible to record more information than has been anticipated by the designer.
- It can be difficult to fill in if sensible instructions are not given.

Menu system

Advantages

- All the possibilities available can be seen at a glance.
- Entry is fast, using just a click.
- It is a user-friendly method – little or no expertise or training is needed.
- The firm does not have to validate the entries – only those on the list are accepted.

Disadvantages

- It is not possible to choose something that is not on the menu.
- If, for example, there are a lot of items for sale, it might not be possible to find the item you want buried in the sub-menus.
- If customers do not find what they want quickly it could put them off.

Natural language

Advantages

- There is no need to learn special commands as 'day-to-day' language is used.
- It is useful for someone with disabilities who cannot use a keyboard.
- No special training is needed to use it.

Disadvantages

- Nuances in language can lead to misunderstandings by the computer.
- It is more difficult to program the computer to accept this interface than other interfaces.

Topic summary

Hardware — input, output, storage devices, specialist hardware.

Software — applications programs, applications packages, systems software, specialist software.

User interfaces — graphical user interface (GUI); command-based or command line interface (CLI); form-based interface; menus; natural language interface; windows, icons, menus, pointers (WIMP) interface.

Standard applications software and systems

1 Basic tasks for types of software

Software can be used for many tasks. Some of them are shown in Figure 3.1. Decide which type of software you would use for each of the following tasks: spreadsheet, database, word processor or presentation package.

Figure 3.1

2 Characteristics of systems

In an examination you will have to look at the key words and the context of the question to know exactly what the examiners want you to write.

The characteristics of a system are a description of the application (the features of the application) and its facilities (what you can do with it).

The application of ICT has come to affect many systems, some of which are listed below. You will be expected to know the characteristics of these systems.

2.1 School administration and teaching systems

A school administration system might consist of:
- an electronic registration system
- a database containing details of the students, including:
  - name
  - address
  - date of birth
  - examination results
  - reports on behaviour and work
  - medical problems

Teachers and students would use computers in many subject areas for writing coursework and researching on the internet. They would use computers in the laboratories for measuring and recording experiments. Some computer-assisted learning (CAL) might be available to some students. Others might use computers in art or music technology, and even in PE lessons students would use videos of themselves to analyse their performance.

Students, teachers and parents might have the facility to view reports and work on the school network from home. There would be web pages advertising the

school and the facility to contact the school by email, send in application details or order items from the school shop. Copies of the school magazine could be available electronically.

2.2 Other example systems

Abbreviated characteristics of some other systems are shown in Table 3.1. You should try to find out more about these systems using the internet, textbooks or your class notes.

System	Description	Facilities
Stock control system	An automatic system used by organisations to help them know how much they have in stock at any time, what needs ordering and how much and what is due to arrive	• Keeps track of goods going out of and coming in to a system • Records the location of stock • Enables automatic reordering of stock • Enables statistical analysis of stock movements, which helps efficient management of the business • Enables 'just in time' ordering, which minimises the storage of stock
Booking system	A system based around a database which can be used to book hotel rooms, flights etc.	• Eliminates 'double booking' • Can be filled in by customers online • Gives fast information on availability • Records customers' data and automatically produces tickets, invoices etc. • Allows multiple inputs from different terminals in any location – useful for companies with many branch offices
Online training system	A system of learning using the help of a computer. Lessons are conducted at a computer terminal. Usually used without a human tutor, but could be coupled with book learning	• Allows lessons to be taken in any order and at the learner's own convenience • Provides tests so the learner can check on his/her progress • Allows management to monitor progress through the training • Can produce an online assessment at the end of the course • Allows the learning to follow the speed of the individual learner • May incorporate sound, video, 'virtual world' simulation
Timetabling and route finding systems	Systems holding details of possible routes and times of travel and used by organisations such as the AA (planning a route from one place to another) and National Rail Enquires (timetabling)	• Allows map printing of planned routes • Allows online searching by customers • Tickets can be produced and printed online • Can give times of travel and alternative routes • Can give instant changes to data for road works/track repairs/accidents/bad weather and so on

System	Description	Facilities
Customer records system	A database of details of the organisation's customers	• Records names and addresses of customers • Records customers' preferences and other information such as age and number of children to help with marketing strategies • May keep records of customers' past purchases • Holds details of customers' preferred payment methods • Records renewal dates for subscriptions • Online systems have methods for customers to alter some data, such as change of address and email address, themselves
Online banking system	A system for customers to manage their bank accounts online and from the comfort of their own homes etc.	• Holds details of customers' accounts which can be viewed by the customer after going through a security login • Is distributed from a secure site to combat hackers • Provides instant statements • Enables customers to move money between accounts electronically, pay bills, set up standing orders • Allows customers to order bank products (e.g. cheque books, insurances, traveller's cheques)

Table 3.1 Characteristics of other systems

3 Wizards and macros

3.1 Wizards

A wizard is usually part of a standard applications package which, by asking the user a series of questions and taking him/her step by step through a process, allows the user to complete a complex task without any expert knowledge. An example is a mail-merge wizard in an 'office'-style application or a chart wizard in a spreadsheet application. A wizard has limited uses, however, as the more expert a user becomes the more confining a wizard becomes, limiting the user's choice and producing results which look much the same as those of every other user of the wizard. The wizard may not produce exactly the result the user wished for.

3.2 Macros

A macro is a sequence of instructions, often written by the user of an application, which reduces a common task to a single key combination or button. Many applications allow the user to record a macro and then assign a key combination, while others allow the user to compile a series of programming instructions to produce the macro.

Examples of macros a user might produce are:

- clearing a section of a spreadsheet
- moving figures on a spreadsheet to a different worksheet
- printing a chart
- placing a letterhead at the top of a page
- running a calculation.

The possibilities for macros are endless.

4 Data entry screens

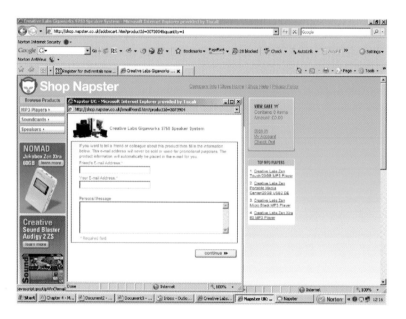

Figure 3.2 Data entry screen

A data entry screen must be designed with great care, as it is often used by inexperienced users. An example of a data entry screen is shown in Figure 3.2. A data entry screen should be set out logically, have an uncluttered screen and have clear instructions with possible online help. Validation of input helps to stop the user entering inappropriate data or accidentally forgetting information, such as the number of items ordered or their date of birth. (The design of the human–computer interface is covered in Topic 9.)

Data entry screens can use a variety of form controls, such as those shown in Table 3.2.

Form control	Description
Forms	Sometimes called a forms dialogue interface, a form contains fields into which the user can type his/her responses.
Menus	Menus allow the designer of the form to give the user a number of options, without expecting the user to know those options in advance. Menus will allow the user to select from a list of actions.
Check boxes	Check boxes allow the user to select items by clicking in a box, which then changes its characteristics.
Radio buttons	Radio buttons limit the user to one choice out of a number. As one button is selected the others become unselected.
Drop-down lists	Drop-down lists allow the designer of the form to limit the choices of the user, such as the months of the year or the colour of a garment. Drop-down lists also help to eliminate spelling mistakes and misunderstandings.
Buttons	Clicking on a clearly labelled button is a simple way of executing a more complex macro, perhaps submitting a completed form, or printing a copy of an order form.

Table 3.2 Form controls in data entry screens

A form control is a point of user interaction.

There are other form controls, such as **text boxes** which allow inputs to a form where they can be validated before entering a system, and **hyperlinks** which when clicked will take the user to another address such as a web page or another page on the same site. A **spinner** will allow a number to be chosen from a fixed incremental list. Some of these form controls are shown in Figure 3.3.

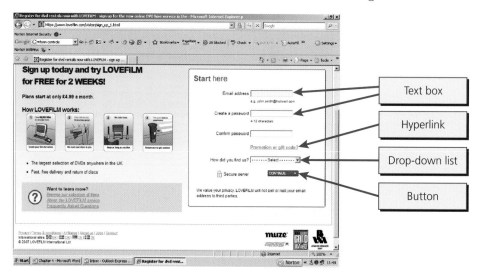

Figure 3.3 Form controls

5 Templates, master documents and corporate identity

Schools have uniforms, school badges and even school songs to try to create a sense of belonging in the students and staff and so that outsiders can recognise members of the school when they see them. Organisations want to give themselves an identity, so that they can be recognised easily by customers and so that members of the organisation feel a sense of belonging with the organisation. To help achieve this an organisation can use templates, style sheets, logos, colours etc. to gain some form of conformity.

5.1 Templates

A template is a standard document with preset layouts (see Figure 3.4). The structure of the document will be already set up, including:

- the text and graphics which are to appear on every document
- the type and size of font
- the margin settings
- the page size
- the landscape or portrait page orientation
- any other formatting details

Using a template means that every time a particular document is produced it will look the same. This is useful for a business, for instance, as it will give a familiar look to its documents which will be recognised by the customer. It also ensures that no important information is left out, and saves time – it is inefficient to have to set up the same headings repeatedly.

Templates can be used for:

- standard letter headings using a word processor
- standard layouts in a spreadsheet
- to produce slides in presentation software that look the same throughout the presentation

Most generic software allows you to save a template.

Company name here   [Click **here** and type return address]

March 14 2008

[Click **here** and type recipient's address]

Dear Sir or Madam:

    Type your letter here. For more details on modifying this letter template, double-click ✉. To return to this letter, use the Window menu.
Sincerely,

[Click **here** and type your name]

[Click **here** and type job title]

Figure 3.4 Example of a company letter template

5.2 House style

Many organisations spend huge amounts of money on publicity, trying to get the public to identify the organisation and associate it with a particular service or as a supplier of particular goods. In order to achieve instant recognition, organisations produce a **corporate identity**. One way of making sure that people recognise the company is to have a **house style** which will involve particular logos, colours and ways of writing.

5.3 Master document

When a number of people in an organisation work together to create a large document, it can be difficult to put the parts together to make a whole. This is where a **master document** comes in. Imagine a group of teachers who are asked to work together to produce a new school prospectus. Each teacher will write about his/her own department or area of interest. A master document can be created and placed on the school network. It will contain all the chapter headings as titles to sub-documents. For example, when the art teacher logs on to write about the art department, the correct sub-document is opened and information can be added. This means the style and format of the whole prospectus can be uniform, the page numbering, headers and footers can be consistent, the table of contents and indexes can be automatically generated and the headteacher can keep control over the whole document. The house style can be preserved throughout the prospectus.

5.4 Master slide

When making a presentation using presentation software, it is important to have a consistent scheme throughout the presentation or the audience will be confused. In addition, continually changing styles of slide will distract from the content. Most organisations giving presentations, for instance a sales manager motivating the sales team, will want to preserve the house style of the organisation. Creating a master slide allows the author of the slides to decide at the outset what fonts, headers, footers etc. to have throughout the presentation and where everything goes.

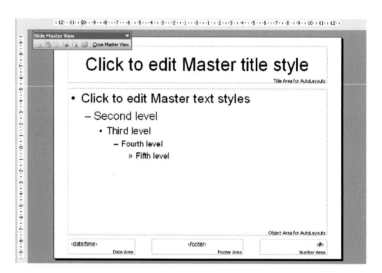

Figure 3.5

5.5 Style sheet

Most organisations create style sheets to help them maintain their house style. A style sheet contains instructions for the layout of a document. Each type of document – letter, memo, report etc. – has its own style sheet. Each style sheet contains instructions for setting up that document, such as which fonts to use, what point size, what should go in the headers and footers, where the logo of the company should be placed and which logo to use.

6 *Transfer of data between applications*

When creating a document using a word processor (for instance when you are working on an A-level project), you might want to import an image or file from another source to include in your document.

It is important for the application to recognise what type of file it is dealing with, so that it can recognise the data held in it and interpret formatting commands, numbers, colours in the images and so on, as each piece of software has its own special way of saving this information. Most standard software can recognise a variety of types of file.

Type of file	File extension
Word file	.doc
Text file	.txt
Image file	.jpg
Spreadsheet file	.xls

Table 3.3 Common types of files

Imagine that you wanted to export a photograph from your photo editor and import it into your word-processed document. Your photo editor uses a special way of saving files and gives them the extension .xyz. Unfortunately, your word processor does not recognise the extension. What do you do? Study Figure 3.6 to see two possible methods.

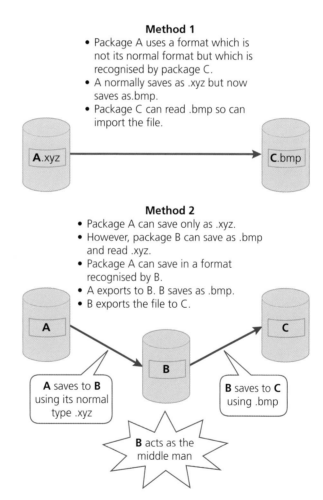

Figure 3.6 Methods of importing files

Topic summary

Characteristics of systems — school administration and teaching systems, stock control, booking systems, online training, timetabling, route finding, customer records, online banking.

Wizards — take the user step by step through a process.

Macros — reduce a sequence of instructions to a single key combination.

Form controls in data entry screens — forms, menus, check boxes, radio buttons, drop-down lists, buttons, text boxes, hyperlinks, spinners.

Templates and master documents — standard documents with preset layouts, used for efficiency and to impose conformity.

Corporate identity — house style, style sheets, logos.

Transfer of data between applications — file types, file extensions, importing files.

Spreadsheet concepts

Learn the purpose and use of worksheets and workbooks.

As with all subjects, spreadsheets come with their own vocabulary. Check that you know what is meant by row, column, cell, workbook and worksheet by looking at the areas labelled in Figure 4.1.

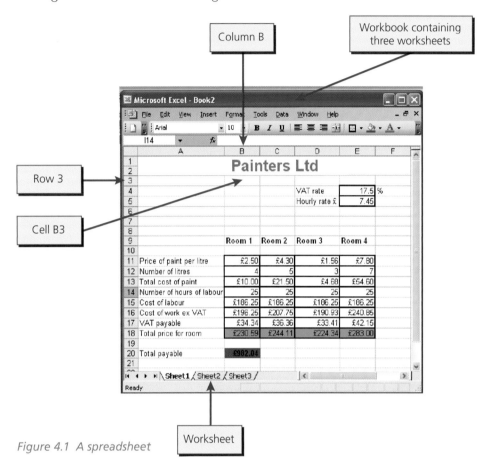

Column B

Workbook containing three worksheets

Row 3

Cell B3

Worksheet

Figure 4.1 A spreadsheet

1 *Worksheets, workbooks and ranges*

1.1 Worksheets

A worksheet is a single page of a spreadsheet. It consists of rows (usually numbered 1, 2, 3 etc.) and columns (usually labelled A, B, C etc.) This arrangement forms many cells, as shown in Figure 4.1. Each cell may contain:
- a number, e.g. 1, 2.65, £3.45
- a formula, e.g. = B3*4, = sum(A1:A12)
- text, e.g. hello

Other features of a spreadsheet or worksheet allow you to:
- format the contents of a cell
- change the width, height and colour of the cell
- construct graphs and charts
- use templates and macros
- use built-in functions such as SUM
- goal seek
- use workbooks
- model situations mathematically

- replicate cells
- create a range of cells and give it a name
- give meaningful names to cells (e.g. instead of B6 write VAT)

The worksheet can be named and can combine with others to become a workbook. Each worksheet can refer to other worksheets in the workbook so that data is interchangeable between them. Usually, if a cell contains a formula it is hidden from view and only the result shows. It is possible to hide cells, columns and rows completely, and to customise the sheet using buttons, menus etc. to make it look attractive and less daunting than the raw sheet. For example, Figure 4.2 shows a spreadsheet calculator which converts pounds sterling to euros and vice versa. The use of buttons makes it look less daunting and makes it practical to use.

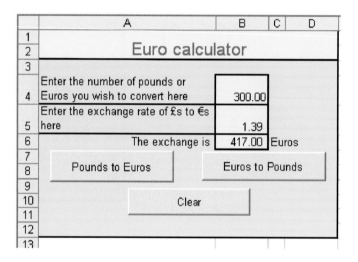

Figure 4.2 A spreadsheet calculator

The purpose of a worksheet is to provide a method for manipulating numbers and formulae in a straightforward manner and in such a way that the cells may be linked by the formulae within them. This can be used for budgets, profit and loss accounts, experimental data or anything based on numbers. It can also be used for mathematical modelling.

1.2 Workbooks

The purpose of a workbook is to increase ease of use by allowing a collection of worksheets to be linked. Cells can be linked across worksheets, and each sheet can be opened from the workbook with a click of the mouse.

A typical use of a workbook would be for a company to keep its accounts of income and expenditure. Each worksheet would be for 1 month and each workbook would be for 1 year.

1.3 Ranges

A range in a spreadsheet is a rectangular set of cells that contains numbers related to a common theme. For instance, the cells might contain the prices of products or student marks from an examination. A range of cells is defined by

the rectangle whose diagonal is the top left-hand cell in the range to the bottom right-hand cell in the range.

The range of cells shaded in Figure 4.3 is defined as B2:C4.

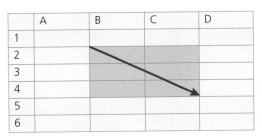

Figure 4.3 A range of cells

Named cells and ranges make spreadsheets more readable.

In the figures below, several ranges have been named to make the spreadsheet more readable. Note that all of Lucy's marks have been called Lucy and all the ICT marks have been called ICT.

The ranges could be called B6:E6 and C4:C7, but Lucy and ICT are easier to read.

	French	ICT	Geography	History	Totals
John	45	56	83	40	224
Fred	67	75	65	79	286
Lucy	83	77	67	65	292
Sanga	71	79	69	70	289
Average	66.5	71.75	71	63.5	

range of cells selected and called Lucy
range of cells selected and called ICT

Instead of the average formula in C9 being AVERAGE(C4:C7) it is now AVERAGE(ICT), which is much more readable.

Figure 4.4 Spreadsheet showing named ranges

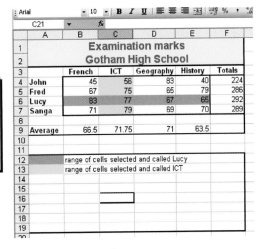

	French	ICT	Geography	History	Totals
John	45	56	83	40	=SUM(John)
Fred	67	75	65	79	=SUM(Fred)
Lucy	83	77	67	65	=SUM(Lucy)
Sanga	71	79	69	70	=SUM(Sanga)
Average	=AVERAGE(French)	=AVERAGE(ICT)	=AVERAGE(Geography)	=AVERAGE(History)	

Figure 4.5 Spreadsheet showing formulae and named ranges

2 Absolute and relative cell referencing

Sometimes when we replicate formulae in a spreadsheet we do not want every cell reference to change. For instance, if VAT is used in a calculation it will stay the same throughout the spreadsheet and will only change if the government decides to change it. We can usually indicate this in a spreadsheet by giving the cell it a name instead of a cell reference (e.g. VAT instead of Z23), or putting $ signs around the cell reference. For instance, reference to cell Z23 would change when replicated down the page to Z24, Z25, Z26 and so on. This is known as **relative referencing**. If we wrote Z23 it would not change and would remain as Z23 as it was replicated. This is known as **absolute referencing**.

Look at spreadsheets A–C in Figure 4.6. They show information for White Goods Ltd and the calculation of VAT on the products.

Spreadsheet A

Spreadsheet B

Spreadsheet C

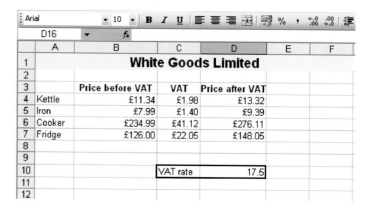

Figure 4.6 Using relative and absolute referencing

Look at column C in Spreadsheet A. We cannot see the formulae used.

In Spreadsheet B, we can see the formulae. VAT has been used as a named cell. This comes from giving the name VAT to cell D10. When the formula is copied from C4 down to C7 that part does not change. This is an example of absolute

referencing. The rest of the formula shows evidence of relative referencing as B4 becomes B5, B5 becomes B6 etc. down the column.

The same spreadsheet is shown in Spreadsheet C, but this time $ signs have been used instead of a name. Throughout column C the reference D10 does not change, though the rest of the formula does.

3 *Spreadsheets and mathematical modelling*

The use of formulae – with changes to one cell leading to changes in all linked cells – is one reason why spreadsheets are so useful for modelling. Spreadsheets are ideal for representing a real-life situation without having to carry out the task in reality. This representation of real life is known as **mathematical modelling** or **simulation**. The model mimics a real system and produces the answers in the form of a graph or a set of numbers. Even in something like a flight simulator, when a trainee pilot feels as though he/she is sitting in a real plane that appears to respond to the controls as a real plane would, it is mathematics controlling it all.

To help with modelling, spreadsheets use the following:
- **Variables** which are used to store data. These might be written as B3, X, C99 etc.
- **Formulae** which are mathematical expressions that are automatically calculated by the spreadsheet and are usually written by the user, e.g. = B3*100/C4.
- **Rules** which are set procedures which must be followed, e.g. IF(H3 = "yes", B4 + 7,B4-7).
- **Functions** which are pre-defined formulae that can be entered into a cell to help carry out a specific function and replace often complex formulae to do common tasks, e.g. SUM, AVERAGE, COUNT, MAX.

3.1 Advantages of modelling software

Modelling is carried out using mathematical methods rather than building models or prototypes of the real thing for a number of reasons. Some of these reasons are shown in the Table 4.1.

Reason	Example
Less dangerous	If you intend to make a manned space flight, or build a bridge across a huge valley, a mathematical model could be used first to see what stresses and strains could be withstood and tested under extreme conditions without putting anyone in danger.
Less expensive	To erect a 100-storey building only to find that it falls down in the event of the first high wind or earth tremor would be extremely costly and dangerous. It is cheaper to try it out mathematically first.
Speeds things up	A scientist wanting to observe the growth of an oak tree under different climate conditions would have to live a long time. Using a model would be much quicker.

Reason	Example
Slows things down	A scientist wishing to observe the movement of particles during an explosion could not actually do so, but enough physics is known to produce a model and to use it to slow events down.
More convenient	It would be inconvenient for the public if the timings of new traffic lights at a road junction were set up incorrectly. To get the most efficient flow of traffic, different timings could be tested using a mathematical model.
Forecasting	It is possible to predict how the future might appear, for example global warming and its effects on sea levels, or the rise in carbon dioxide linked to cutting down and burning forests.
Ease of use	A mathematical model is piece of software, so it can be saved on disc, emailed, shared over a network and backed up safely.

Table 4.1 Reasons for using modelling software

3.2 Exploring ideas with modelling

Models are usually created using a variety of factors. If you want to create a model of a section of road to improve its design, for example to slow traffic in a housing estate, you would need to use:

- **observed facts**, e.g. how many motorists use a particular stretch of road at a particular time
- **random numbers**, e.g. to simulate different vehicles or vehicle speeds or weather conditions
- **established formulae**, e.g. formulae for speed, acceleration, stopping distances
- **rules created for the model**, e.g. the maximum speed is 30 mph, the bumps cannot be more than 20 cm high

You would then try out the model under different conditions by changing the variables and observing the results. The speed bumps can vary in the model from 0 to 20 cm high. We can assess the conditions using a **what if question**: 'What if the speed bumps were 15 cm high?' As many what ifs as necessary can be asked until the model gives a satisfactory answer and the design and implementation of the plan can go ahead.

An **hypothesis** is when an answer is predicted and the model is used to see if the answer is correct. For instance, in the speed bump example above, an hypothesis could be: 'If three speed bumps, 5 cm high, are placed 20 cm apart, they will slow the average speed of cars by 10 mph.' The model could be used to test this hypothesis.

Goal seeking is when the model is used 'back to front'. The desired outcome is stated and the model works out what values the variables should have been to reach that outcome. For instance: 'If three speed bumps are placed 20 cm apart, how high should they be to slow the average speed of cars by 10 mph?'

3.3 Disadvantages of modelling and simulation

The outcome of any modelling process is only as good as the model. If formulae, assumptions or rules are incorrect then the outcome of the model will be incorrect. All models should be tested against known outcomes to make sure that they work. Predictions using models are not always reliable, since it may not be possible to take into account every factor, factors may not be known, or they may change. For example, a perfect model for deciding where to put speed bumps may be created, but tyre manufacturers may then produce a speed-bump-shock-absorbing tyre which everyone starts using, thus raising the average speed again.

Remember:

- A simulation may oversimplify complex problems or fail to take into account all variables.
- The problem may not have been fully understood.
- There is a tendency for over-reliance on the outcome and human judgement is clouded by the thought that 'computers are always right'. Using simulations can take away an element of common sense.

Topic summary

Spreadsheets — row, column, cell, worksheet, workbook, range.

Cell referencing — absolute, relative.

Spreadsheets and mathematical modelling — variables, formulae, rules, functions, hypothesis, goal seeking.

1 Database terminology

Learn these definitions.

A database is a large collection of data. The data can be accessed by a number of applications. You you will need to learn the terminology related to databases shown in Table 5.1.

A **flat file database** is one in which the data is held in a single table, about a single subject, consisting of rows and columns. It has limited use as it is confined to the data in that one table.

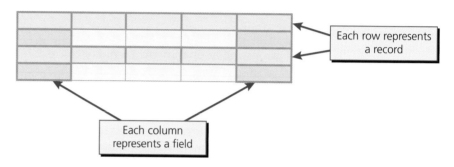

Figure 5.1 A flat file database

A **relational database** is a more complex structure with stored pointers linking related data items. Because it is possible to set up links to form new relationships, without changing or adding more data, a relational database is a powerful and useful tool.

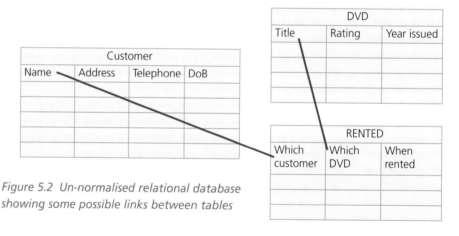

Figure 5.2 Un-normalised relational database showing some possible links between tables

Term	Description
Table	A table is a part of the relational database which concerns a particular topic, such as BORROWERS or BOOKS. For instance, the table of borrowers in Figure 5.3 only contains data about the borrowers, not the books they have borrowed.
Record	A record is part of a table. It is all the data relating to a particular member of the table, in this case all the data about a particular borrower.
Entity	An entity is another name for table. The total set of records in this table make up the entity called BORROWER.

Term	Description
Field	A field is an individual section of the record which contains data about one aspect of the record. In this case, a field is one piece of information about the borrower, such as date of birth or first name.
Attribute	An attribute is another name for field. A set of fields, each containing the same attribute of an entity, form a column in the table. Each member (or record) of the entity makes a row in the table.
Primary key/key field	One of the fields in any record must be able to distinguish that record from all others in the table. In the BORROWERS table, in each attribute there is data which is the same: two Johns, two Browns, lots of Mytowns. This usually happens when a table is constructed, so an extra attribute is created, usually called something like BorrowerID. This could be a unique number for each customer, and will form the key field or primary key for that record.
Foreign key	When a key field of one table appears in another table in the database.
Composite key/key field	Sometimes it is necessary to use two or more foreign keys to create a composite key field for a table. Imagine the situation in a library. A table holds details of who has what book. Each book can only be borrowed by one person at a time, but each person could have more than one book out. Each borrower has a unique primary key, each book has a unique primary key, so in the borrowed book table these two keys become foreign keys that can be united to form a unique composite key.
Relationship	In a relational database, tables are joined using relationships. These relationships can be: • one to one • one to many • many to many This is discussed in more detail below.
Redundant data	Redundant data happens when the data which has been put into a field could have been produced by using values from other fields in the database.
Referential integrity	If a database has referential integrity it means that any data referred to by another table actually exists. Imagine that a person borrows a book, but then leaves the library. If the person's details were removed from the table containing library member details, this part of the foreign key in the borrowed book table would point to nothing. The table would not have referential integrity (see below Figure 5.4).
Duplicate data	If the borrower details were recorded in other tables in the database this would waste space, since only the borrower primary key is required as a foreign key in the new table. Such duplication could also lead to errors, for example if one table was updated with a change of telephone number but this was not changed in other tables.

Table 5.1 Database technology

	FirstName	LastName	Address1	Address2	PostCode	Telephone	DoB
TABLE or ENTITY							
	John	Smith	1 Maple Ave	Mytown	MT1 1XY	102342	120145
Field	John	Brown	The Cottage	Mytown	MT2 2BC	123456	311253
	Margaret	White	2 Sunshine View	Mytown	MT1 1XY	143212	231219
Record	Sanga	Black	Long Lane	Mytown	MT3 7FF	234567	290284
	Phil	Green	Windmills	Mytown	MT2 2BC	765432	111165
	Jim	Turner	DunRoam in	Mytown	MT1 3JN	564534	020752
	Fred	Weaver	Thistledo	Mytown	MT3 3AB	789708	241151
	Lucy	Brown	6 Orchard Close	Mytown	MT1 1RT	100034	020752
	Sunil	French	14 Main Street	Mytown	MT2 6GT	907876	111057
	Ben	Kent	The Cottage	Mytown	MT2 2BC	123456	090988
							Attribute

Figure 5.3 Table of borrowers for a library

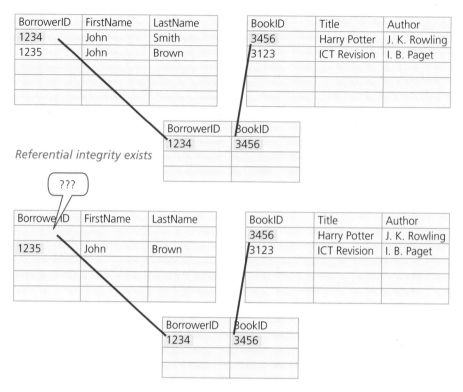

Figure 5.4 John Smith is removed and referential integrity is lost

2   *The data dictionary*

When a database is being designed, a data dictionary is created to help people building or maintaining the database. It contains all the information needed concerning the data within the database and the structure of the data. Data dictionaries are sometimes called data directories.

Typically, a data dictionary will hold the following information:
- names of tables (entities) unique to each table
- names of fields (attributes) unique to each field
- data types (Boolean, real, text etc.)
- data lengths (how many characters are allowed, where relevant)
- restrictions (is it a closed list or between an upper and lower limit?)
- data validation on input fields (validation methods were studied in Topic 1)
- relationships (between the tables)
- key fields (every entity must have a primary key)
- permissions as to who can change data
- indexed fields

3   *Relationships between entities*

When tables (entities) are linked, the links can take one of three types. Some simple examples are given below:
- **One to one**
  - one person in one seat at the cinema for a particular performance
  - a particular book is borrowed by a particular person at a certain time
  - one person has one National Insurance number

- **One to many or many to one**
  - one person borrows many books
  - many fines can be given to one person
- **Many to many**
  - many customers order many products
  - many books are borrowed by many people

3.1 Entity relationship diagrams

Relationships can be shown diagrammatically.

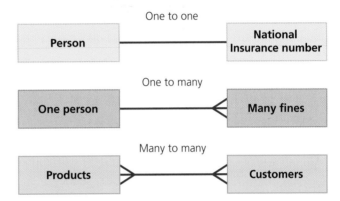

Figure 5.5

Many-to-many relationships are difficult to deal with when using databases, so they are usually changed by inserting a third table between the two entities with the many-to-many relationship.

For instance, in the library example, an individual book borrowed by an individual borrower on a certain date can be identified as shown below.

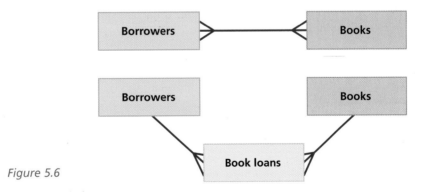

Figure 5.6

---

4 ## Normalisation of a database

Imagine a company that sells computer equipment to customers all over the world. An order form sent to the warehouse could contain the following information:

- customer ID number
- the name of the customer
- the address of the customer
- the ID of the equipment
- a description of the equipment

A customer called Ian Barry puts in an order for a number of items. The order form to the warehouse might contain the following information.

- 123, Ian Barry, 1234 Last Street, Gloucester, GL12XX, England, 78, hard drive
- 123, Ian Barry, 1234 Last Street, Gloucester, GL12XX, England, 93, scanner
- 123, Ian Barry, 1234 Last Street, Gloucester, GL12XX, England, 56, printer
- 123, Ian Barry, 1234 Last Street, Gloucester, GL12XX, England, 121, printer cartridge

The company could record data like this in a database, but it would be inefficient.

Before entities are created and relationships set, a database needs to be **normalised**.

4.1 Advantages of normalisation

Normalisation of a database helps the database to be robust and queries to produce sensible answers. When a relational database is normalised:

- no redundant data will appear in the final tables
- duplicate data is reduced
- referential integrity is preserved
- the consistency of the data is increased
- every entity and attribute is clearly defined
- the database is easier to maintain
- there is greater flexibility for future expansion

4.2 Characteristics of first, second and third normal form

Until normalisation is carried out, the data is known as **un-normalised data** or data in **0NF**. To put the database into **first normal form (1NF)** we must first make sure that the fields are **atomic** – we cannot break them down further. We must also remove repeating attributes – fields that contain the same data repeated. A database with no repeating attributes or repeating groups of attributes, and in which all data is atomic, is in first normal form (1NF).

Table 5.2 shows some of the data collected to go in the computer company database. At the moment it is in 0NF, so we need to normalise it. There are repeating attributes – Ian Barry, appears in every entry. In addition, the data is not atomic.

Process of normalisation

Check the data is atomic. The name field is non-atomic, because Ian Barry is two separate names. The address field is also non-atomic. Making the data atomic gives the following list of attributes:

CustomerID	Postcode
FirstName	Country
LastName	EquipmentID
Address1	Description
Town	

Customer ID	Name	Address	Equipment ID	Equipment description
123	Ian Barry	1234 Last Street Gloucester GL12XX England	78	hard drive
123	Ian Barry	1234 Last Street Gloucester GL12XX England	93	scanner
123	Ian Barry	1234 Last Street Gloucester GL12XX England	56	printer
123	Ian Barry	1234 Last Street Gloucester GL12XX England	121	printer cartridge

Table 5.2 Data collected for database

Choose a primary key. The starting point is to choose a primary key on which to base the first table. Since the main aim of the database is to record details about the customer, the CustomerID is the primary key.

Remove repeating data to another entity. The repeating data are the customer's name and address. Move these repeating attributes to make a second entity, leaving the first entity with only EquipmentID and Description. Record these entities in a standard format.

A link between EQUIPMENT and CUSTOMER must be maintained. This link is CustomerID.

In 1NF this database now consists of:

> FIRST_ENTITY (EquipmentID, CustomerID, Description)
> SECOND_ENTITY (CustomerID, FirstName, LastName, Address1,Town, Postcode, Country)

The database is still not normalised. The next stage is to move to **second normal form** or **2NF**.

The characteristics of 2NF are that the database is in 1NF and there are no partial dependencies. Each attribute must rely entirely on the full key field for that entity.

Check for partial dependencies. In FIRST_ENTITY the key field is a composite key made by combining EquipmentID and CustomerID. The Description field only relies on part of this key so can be moved out to make a third entity, leaving this FIRST_ENTITY in 2NF.

There are no partial key dependencies in SECOND_ENTITY. This leads to:

    FIRST_ENTITY(EquipmentID, CustomerID)
    SECOND_ENTITY(CustomerID, FirstName, LastName, Address1,Town,
    Postcode, Country)
    THIRD_ENTITY(EquipmentID, Description)

The database may still not be normalised. The next stage is to move to **third normal form** or **3NF**. The characteristics of 3NF are that the database is in 2NF and there are no non-key dependencies. All fields relate directly to the primary key field of that entity.

In our example, all fields do relate to the primary key in each case so the database is now in 3NF. All that remains is to give the entities sensible names:

    ORDER_ITEM (EquipmentID, CustomerID)
    CUSTOMER (CustomerID, FirstName, LastName, Address1,Town,
    Postcode, Country)
    EQUIPMENT (EquipmentID, Description)

Here is another example. DVDRents2U hires out DVDs to customers. The following information needs to appear in the database:

    CustomerID
    Name of customer
    Address of customer
    Telephone name of customer
    Date of birth of customer
    DVDID
    Title of each DVD
    Year DVD was issued
    Rating of each DVD (PG, 18 etc.)
    Date on which DVD was hired

A customer may rent many DVDs.

Putting the database into first normal form (1NF), repeating attributes are removed. This leaves two sets of attributes:

    CustomerID
    DVDID
    Title of each DVD
    Year DVD was issued
    Rating of each DVD (PG,18 etc.)
    Date on which DVD was hired

    CustomerID
    Name of customer
    Address of customer
    Telephone name of customer
    Date of birth of customer

Make the data atomic. The first set of data is fine, so we can call it FIRST_ENTITY and write it in conventional form:

> FIRST_ENTITY (DVDID, CustomerID, DVDTitle, YearIssued, Rating, DateHired)

SECOND_ENTITY has to be changed as the name and address data are non-atomic:

> SECOND_ENTITY (CustomerID, FirstName, LastName, Address1, Address2, Telephone, DateOfBirth)

To go into 2NF, look for partial key dependencies.

In FIRST_ ENTITY, DVDTitle, YearIssued and Rating are only related to part of the key so move them to THIRD_ENTITY.

For 2NF we now have:

> FIRST_ENTITY (DVDID, CustomerID, DateHired)
> SECOND_ENTITY (CustomerID, FirstName, LastName, Address1, Address2, Telephone, DateOfBirth)
> THIRD_ENTITY (DVDID, DVDTitle, YearIssued, Rating)

For 3NF, look for non-key dependencies. All attributes in each entity in the example now depend completely on the primary key of that entity, so they are in 3NF without further change. Give the entities sensible names, and we have the basis of a good database:

> RENTING (DVDID, CustomerID, DateHired)
> CUSTOMER (CustomerID, FirstName, LastName, Address1, Address2, Telephone, DateOfBirth)
> DVD (DVDID, DVDTitle, YearIssued, Rating)

5 Searches and parameters

One function of useful databases is that they can be searched using queries. There are many types of query, some of which are shown below.

A **simple query** finds information from one or more tables based on the search for one field. For example, in the database above we could search for all DVDs with the rating 18.

A **complex query** searches on more than one parameter using Boolean operators such as AND, OR, NOT and may be based on attributes from more than one entity. For example, we could search for all customers who have rented DVDs rated certificate 18 AND who like horror films.

A **dynamic parameter query** is where the user has to provide the parameter at the start of the search. If a customer asks if a particular DVD is in stock, the shop assistant has to type in that DVD name before the search can take place.

A **static parameter query** contains the pre-defined parameters for the search. For example, the owner of the business may wish to print out a list of all DVDs issued more than 3 years ago for a sale of out-of-date discs. The query will already contain the parameter 3, which is used every time the query is run.

Topic summary

Database — flat file, relational.

Database terms — table, record, entity, field, attribute, primary key/key field, foreign key, composite key, relationship, redundant data, referential integrity, duplicate data.

Data dictionary — the information needed to help people create or maintain the database.

Relationships between entities — one to one, one to many, many to one, many to many, entity relationship diagrams.

Normalisation — first, second and third normal forms.

Searches and parameters — simple and complex queries, dynamic and static parameter queries.

TOPIC **6** Presentation and communication of data

1 *Characteristics of documents*

There are a number of specialist terms used to describe the characteristics of documents. Many of these are shown and described in Figure 6.1.

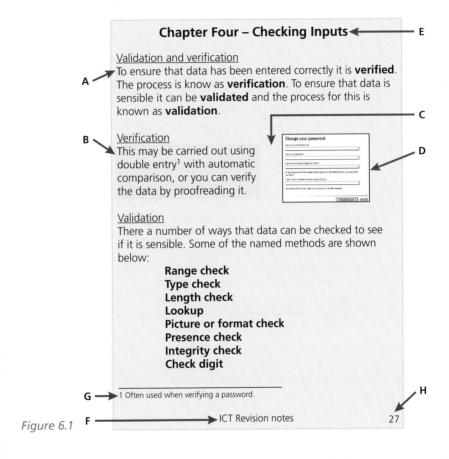

Chapter Four – Checking Inputs ◄——— E

Validation and verification
A ——► To ensure that data has been entered correctly it is **verified**. The process is know as **verification**. To ensure that data is sensible it can be **validated** and the process for this is known as **validation**.

———— C

Verification
B ——► This may be carried out using double entry[1] with automatic comparison, or you can verify the data by proofreading it.

——► D

Validation
There a number of ways that data can be checked to see if it is sensible. Some of the named methods are shown below:

> **Range check**
> **Type check**
> **Length check**
> **Lookup**
> **Picture or format check**
> **Presence check**
> **Integrity check**
> **Check digit**

G ——► 1 Often used when verifying a password.

——► H

F ————————► ICT Revision notes   27

Figure 6.1

Some examples of characters not normally found on the keyboard include © ¢ Δ ≠.

A Character – usually anything you can type with the keyboard, though there may be some special characters which you have to get from a character map.

B Paragraph – a short passage or collection of sentences about a particular topic, usually separated from other paragraphs by a blank line.

C Section – a section in a document defines an area which has particular formatting. When a new section is introduced the formatting may change, for example from a portrait to a landscape page layout, or from 2 columns to 3 columns.

D Frame – a frame defines an area that can be moved around the page. It can contain text and graphics, and these will not be disturbed when the frame is moved.

E Header – text that appears in an area specially reserved for it (known as a header margin) at the top of a document.

F Footer – text that appears in an area specially reserved for it (known as a footer margin) at the bottom of a document.

G **Footnote** – a reference or comment at the foot of a page, often linked with a superscript numeral.

H **Page** – a section of a document separated from other sections by a page break. These breaks can be hard breaks, introduced by the user before the natural end to a page, or soft breaks, which are automatically generated by the software depending on the page size. Page numbers can be automatically placed in the header or footer by the software.

2 Reformatting documents to meet the needs of an application

Documents are used every day by most businesses and organisations. The documents could be letters, application forms, invoices, receipts and so on. Documents are often reformatted to meet the needs of an application. For instance, when a doctor writes a prescription it is reformatted by the pharmacist to make a label to stick on the medicine. Both documents contain basically the same information but the label is in a different format for a different purpose. When a worksheet is written for an A-level ICT group it might be reformatted to a different font size for a partially-sighted student.

3 Mail merge

Information held by a company on a database or spreadsheet, such as a customer's name and address or the amount of money they owe, can be used together with a word processor to produce a **standard letter**. This type of letter contains a set wording, but the personal details such as name and address can be changed automatically for each customer by using the information found in the database or spreadsheet. This process is known as **mail merge**.

The process can be summarised as follows:
- A standard document is created using the word processor.
- A data source is created using the database or spreadsheet.
- The standard document is merged with the data source and/or details from the spreadsheet to produce a personalised document.
- The document is printed.

DTP packages can also be used for mail merge.

Advantages of using mail merge:
- The standard letter only needs to be written once and can then be used without manual interference.
- The letter can be saved and used again in similar circumstances, which is quicker than having to create it from scratch.
- The letter only needs to be proofread once.
- The same data source can be used for other standard letters.

Disadvantages of using mail merge:
- People dislike receiving letters they perceive as 'junk mail'.
- Silly mistakes can occur if the database is not carefully maintained, such as letters being sent to 'Dear Mr Deceased, or Dear Mrs BA (Hons). In one case, 20,000 letters were sent to the same person when the process went wrong.

4 ## Clipart and thumbnail images

Documents often contain small pictures known as **clipart**. It is possible to buy sets of these images, known as **libraries**.

The images can be viewed quickly using **thumbnails** which are small versions of the images. For instance, in kitchen design a number of images of fitted units, cookers, washing machines etc. can be kept in a library of images. When the designer is designing the kitchen the images can be viewed, selected and inserted into the design. Similarly, in cartography (the production of maps) and in network design, the appropriate images can be found in libraries.

Using image libraries also has disadvantages. Unless you created the library yourself, the images will not be unique to your organisation. Clipart is often basic and varies in quality.

5 ## Bitmap and vector graphics

A pixel or picture element is one dot of a graphic which is a particular colour.

Bitmap graphics are made of **pixels**. Each pixel has a position and a colour and is usually square. Many thousands of these dots are grouped together and to the human eye they appear to be connected. However, the larger the image the more dots are needed to maintain quality, and the size of the image in computer memory terms becomes huge. If small graphics are enlarged the image becomes 'pixilated' – as the individual pixels get bigger, the image becomes distorted.

Vector graphics are made of points which are described by their relative distance from the point of origin in the form of equations. Components are described by length, thickness and colour. Because the points are generated mathematically, the images can be scaled up without loss of quality.

6 ## Features of presentation software

Presentation software, for instance Microsoft PowerPoint, is often used to help with teaching or lecturing, or as an automatic display of slides at an exhibition, in a shop window or the entrance foyer to an office. A set of slides is created, each one capable of containing text, images, sound or video. Various effects can alter the way that the information appears on the screen. This is known as **slide animation**.

Table 6.1 lists the features of presentation software.

Feature	Description
Text	Words, characters or numbers
Image	A picture or cartoon
Sound	A clip of music, voice etc.
Video	A clip of moving pictures
Animation	Movement of the text or other objects on the page
Slide transition	Special effects that occur when one slide changes for another
Hyperlink	A link which, when clicked, will move to another part of the presentation or to somewhere outside the presentation
Hotspot	An area on the screen that will respond to a click of the mouse
Button	Like a hotspot, a button responds to a mouse click to allow the user to move to another slide or introduce a special effect

Table 6.1 Features of presentation software

6.1 Presentation software versus OHP

It is sometimes useful to use OHP slides for a presentation; sometimes it is better to use presentation software. Table 6.2 gives some advantages and disadvantages of each method.

Presentation method	Advantages	Disadvantages
OHP	<ul><li>Does not rely on a computer.</li><li>No special computer training needed.</li><li>May be more reliable than a computer.</li><li>Less equipment to carry round.</li><li>Hard copy is readily available.</li><li>You can write on the transparencies during the presentation.</li></ul>	<ul><li>More difficult to standardise the slides.</li><li>Cannot easily be saved to disc.</li><li>More difficult to edit and to change the order.</li><li>If the set of slides is dropped it can become out of order.</li><li>Difficult to include special effects such as sound, video or animation.</li></ul>
Presentation software	<ul><li>Easy to standardise the slides.</li><li>Can be saved to disc/memory stick.</li><li>Easy to edit and to change the order.</li><li>Will not be dropped and become out of order.</li><li>You can include special effects, sound, video and animation.</li></ul>	<ul><li>Relies on a computer.</li><li>Training is needed to use the computer.</li><li>Computers can sometimes be unreliable and crash or not connect to the projector.</li><li>More expensive equipment to carry around.</li><li>Difficult to annotate the slides during a presentation.</li></ul>

Table 6.2 Advantages and disadvantages of presentation methods

6.2 Automatic and manual transition of slides

Automatic transmission of slides is when the presentation is set to run continuously without human intervention. This is useful in situations such as a museum display where the presentation describes a particular exhibit or at a school speech day where a presentation details the achievements made by the school during the previous year. Automatic presentation does, however, have disadvantages. It might move too slowly (or too quickly) to satisfy the audience. It might break down without anyone noticing. It is not possible to ask questions or to receive further information about a particular slide.

Manual transmission is when the presenter moves the slides on by clicking a mouse or pressing a button on a remote hand-held device. This method is useful when the presenter is engaging with the audience, answering questions and pausing the presentation to expand on a point made. The main disadvantage of manual transition is that a speaker has to be present.

6.3 Linear, non-linear and hierarchical presentations

A **linear presentation** is where one slide follows another in a set order.

A **non-linear presentation** – or mesh presentation – allows jumping from slide to slide in any order.

A **hierarchical presentation** allows alternative routes through the presentation. It follows a linear route within each 'tree'.

Advantages and disadvantages of each method are given in Table 6.3.

Presentation method	Advantages	Disadvantages
Linear	• Follows a pre-defined order so arguments can be developed logically. • Suitable for an automatic slide show.	• Lack of flexibility. • Presenter-based rather than audience-based.
Non-linear	• Can take a unique path through the slides each time to satisfy audience needs.	• Can be confusing to both audience and presenter.
Hierarchical	• Can follow the interests of the audience. • Can branch to different topics easily. • Good for an experienced audience who wish to be involved in discussion.	• May need to return to the menu slide each time the presenter takes a different path.

Table 6.3 Presentation types

Topic summary

Characteristics of documents — character, paragraph, section, frame, header, footer, footnote, page.

Mail merge — using information held on a database or spreadsheet together with a word processor to produce a standard letter.

Graphics — clipart, thumbnails, bitmap, vector.

Presentation software — features; automatic transmission; manual transmission; linear, non-linear and hierarchical presentations.

The role and impact of ICT

1 The impact of ICT on society, organisations and individuals

ICT has had a huge impact on society and many of the developments affect our lives at work, home and in our leisure time. As you move about your house, you will find ICT in your mobile phone, computer, television, MP3 player, microwave oven and washing machine. Your central heating system runs with the aid of ICT. When you leave your home, the car or bus you use will almost certainly have a computer-monitored engine. There may be satellite navigation installed and a radio/CD player. Your supermarket has tills monitored by ICT. Your bank is controlled by ICT. Everything you pay for by a credit or debit card depends on ICT. It is, in fact, almost impossible for ICT not to impinge on your life on a daily basis. It is important to keep up to date with these developments and to question any development we might perceive as being bad for individuals or society in general.

Of course, there are advantages to most advances in ICT, e.g. developments in the fields of communication and medicine. However, some people are worried about the rapid advances in ICT and laws have been introduced in most countries around the world to protect us from fraud, damage, dishonesty and health risks related to ICT. Not all countries have high standards, however, and so you must be on your guard when using a computer linked to the internet as this is effectively an entry into your home or office from any part of the globe. There are also concerns about our society's dependence on ICT and whether we could function effectively without it. You may think that the advantages outweigh the disadvantages, but we must never let our enthusiasm for embracing new technology blind us to possible problems.

Some developments where ICT has had a day-to-day impact on our lives are in transport, medicine, helping the disabled, education, entertainment, shopping, marketing and communication.

1.1 Transport

- **Global positioning systems (GPS)** allow individuals, such as cyclists, to know exactly where they are or receive directions to their destination using a small device which picks up satellite signals and displays maps and instructions.
- **Speed limiters** are fitted to engines to prevent vehicles exceeding a certain speed limit, making the roads safer and lessening fuel consumption.
- **Emission controllers** are fitted to engines to reduce the amount of carbon dioxide entering the atmosphere.
- **Traffic congestion zones** limit the number of vehicles entering city centres. In London, CCTV cameras can read number plates of vehicles entering the zone and automatically check if the vehicle owners have paid the congestion charge. If they have not paid, a fine is automatically sent to the owner using the DVLA database.

1.2 Medicine

- **Sensors**, both analogue and digital, are used extensively in medicine for readings and data collection. Many developments have enabled heartbeat, blood pressure, blood sugar levels and even the particles in a person's breath to be checked automatically and data to be recorded for later analysis. Having sensors monitoring patients frees up medical staff to do other work. In an emergency the devices will sound an alarm to summon staff.
- **Scanning devices** have made the work of diagnosing illness easier than having to invade a body by surgery to discover what is going on inside:
  - *Magnetic resonance imaging (MRI)*. Using a strong magnetic field, differences in body tissues can be detected. This is ideal for scanning brains, muscles and other soft tissue areas.
  - *Computerised axial tomography (CAT)*. This is commonly known as a CAT scan. It uses a combination of X-rays and computers to produce three-dimensional images of structures within a body, so that blood clots, tumours or fractures can be located. It can even be used to look at the density of a person's bones or for infection within the body.
  - *Ultrasound*. Using high-frequency sound waves and computers to generate images, parts of the body can be investigated without physical invasion. This method is most commonly associated with images of unborn babies.
- **Backup and recovery** procedures ensure that vital medical data is not lost if anything goes wrong with the computer system at a hospital and that patient records and notes of treatments administered are not lost.
- **Electronic patient record-keeping (EPR)** allows data to be shared quickly by medical staff and has the advantage of not being subject to misunderstanding, e.g. bad handwriting. It also allows rapid searching of the data, e.g. if there was a worry about a particular drug then the information on every patient who had been prescribed that drug could be found quickly.
- **Blood barcoding** and tracking systems have been developed to ensure patient safety during treatment. This method should avoid problems such as the wrong blood type being used in a transfusion or penicillin being administered to a patient who is allergic to it. A unique barcode is generated for a patient. At every stage during a medical procedure the barcodes of drugs and blood to be administered are cross-checked by a computer against the patient's barcode. Any problems are immediately flagged up by the computer and adjustments can be made by the medical staff.
- Use of the **internet, intranets and extranets** (see Topic 10) enable the rapid sharing of information concerning patients, treatments and medicines.
- **Distributed medical databases** are discussed in more detail in Topic 11.

1.3 Specialist equipment for disabled people

- **Specialist hardware** has been created which allows people with many different types of disability to access a computer. People with loss of manual function could use an eye-typer, a puff-suck switch, a mouth-stick or a foot mouse as inputs to the computer (see Topic 2). Those with a visual impairment can have work printed out by a Braille embosser.

- **Specialist software**, such as speech synthesisers for the visually impaired or artificial intelligence completing words, enable people who cannot use their fingers on a keyboard to enter words more quickly.
- **Artificial limbs** can be joined to the nervous system of the human body and function almost as a real limb. Feedback from an artificial hand can let the brain know the pressure with which the object is being held, allowing the user to pick up an egg without breaking it, for example. Pacemakers and other devices which have an ICT element have enabled people with certain disabilities to be more independent and to integrate more effectively into society.
- **Artificial retinas** can enhance sight while hearing can be enhanced with devices hidden inside the ear.

1.4 Education
- **Computer-aided learning (CAL)**, or **computer-based training (CBT)**, has many advantages, such as allowing learners to work at their own pace and in their own time. The software provides information in small amounts and asks the student questions. The software then responds to the student's answers. Work can be repeated as often as necessary and has the advantage, from an employer's point of view, that it can be monitored as a record of the work the student is doing and the student's success rate is recorded by the computer. Students can also use **revision programs** designed to test learning on a particular subject, which often include feedback and 'Help links' in a similar fashion to CAL.
- **Distance learning** uses the computer and a network, often the internet, to take part in classes and attend lectures or conferences and discussions using video-conferencing techniques. A well-known example is the work done by the Open University, where anyone in the world is able to take a degree course without attending an actual university, using a combination of the computer, DVD/CD player and textbooks. Assignments can be submitted electronically and the feedback from the tutors arrives in the same way.
- **Video-conferencing** allows people who are separated geographically to hold a meeting or conference by using webcams, microphones, speakers, computers and networks such as the internet. This is useful in education (e.g. the Open University) or for business. The advantage of video-conferencing is that no one has to travel, so jet-lag and travel expenses are avoided and a lot of travelling time is saved.
- **E-learning** means electronic learning. The 'e' is often used in expressions where the computer plays a major part, such as e-commerce, e-business, e-mail, e-marketing, and e-sales. E-learning is any kind of instruction or learning that takes place using the computer. This includes CAL, CBT and distance learning.
- **Chat** is software that allows users to communicate interactively using the internet. One method of allowing several users to communicate together is **internet relay chat (IRC)**. Areas set aside for particular discussions are called 'chat rooms'. This is an ideal way for distance learning students to hold discussions with tutors or experts in a particular field without having to travel to meet them.

- **Authoring software**, sometimes referred to as authoring language or authoring tools, allows a teacher to write CAL packages while concentrating on the educational aspects of the work rather than worrying about how the computer will deal with it. The teacher can input questions and answers, and decide what work will be displayed, including text, video and sound clips. Authoring software can also be used for writing web pages if the author is not familiar with HTML.

- **Interactive whiteboards** are often seen in schools. They are a combination of a whiteboard and a projector linked to a computer. The teacher can use a virtual pen or eraser to write on the board, project images directly from the computer or internet, or use a combination of these. It is a versatile and clean method of providing information during lessons.

- **Computer-based methods of registration** are being used increasingly in schools. Many ideas are being trialled. One method is that each teacher has a laptop computer and as students arrive for a particular lesson the teacher records this on the laptop, which is linked via a wireless network to the school office. This is a two-way process and the office can alert the teacher if a student is absent, will miss a lesson for some reason, or has been disruptive in earlier lessons. Another method is to issue each student with a registration smart-card which can be swiped on entering or leaving the school or classroom, thus registering their presence or absence with the central system. Cards with barcodes could be used in a similar way (many libraries make use of this technology).

- **Registration** or enrolment on courses at schools, colleges and universities can be carried out online. This process means that students can register for courses without having to travel to a central location, which is cheaper and more efficient for the administrators of the educational establishment. This process is known as **online module registration (OMR)** and should not be confused with Optical Mark Readers, also known as OMR.

- Many schools now allow or encourage students to use **laptop computers** to access and carry out their work in schools. This relies on a suitable **wireless network system** being available in the school and a sufficiently high level of security to keep the students' and the school's data safe.

- **Smart cards** are swipe-cards with a microchip embedded in them which is capable of remembering certain facts and adjusting that memory. Used in conjunction with a smart card reader and a computer system, it is capable of many useful services. Students could be issued with smart cards for use in the school canteen, which could keep track of how much money they spend, as well as ensuring that students eat a balanced diet and avoid buying food which may contain substances they are allergic to. The card could also be used in other shops around the school, for registration in classes and in the school library.

- **Student record-keeping** can be carried out using a combination of the registration techniques described above and a database. Alongside personal details such as name and address, results from examinations and which examination board was used can be stored as well as details such as effort and special achievements such as sport or music. Ideally, if students have to move from one school to another, their record can go with them.

What next?

Retina scans – it has been discovered that each person has a unique pattern on their retina which can be recorded on a computer. If students have their retinas scanned at the beginning of 0 course they could be scanned again when they entered an examination hall. This would ensure that no student could substitute for another in the examinations. Retina scans could be used for student registration, which would avoid the problem of lost registration or swipe-cards. However, there are problems associated with privacy that still need resolving.

1.5 Entertainment

ICT is found in many areas of entertainment. Some are so well known they need no further expansion here, such as:

- games
- photography – taking digital photographs and editing them using appropriate software
- mobile phones
- music, including downloading from the internet
- email
- interactive services, e.g. betting, voting, dating
- cinema and theatre booking

Other uses of ICT include:

- **Musical instrument digital interface (MIDI)** allows musical data to pass from an instrument to the computer or vice versa. MIDI is a well-accepted standard, which means that the codes used to transfer the music are used by all manufacturers. Instruments from different manufacturers can be used with any musical software that adheres to the MIDI standard.
- **Sequencers** can be used in music synthesisers and drum machines. They are digital devices capable of storing notes, chords and samples of music which can be played through multiple tracks. Music can be entered into a sequencer using **real-time** by playing the instrument and having the sequencer pick it up, or using **step-time** entry where each note is entered separately by the user.
- A **notator** is a piece of software that allows MIDI files to be displayed in traditional note form for printing and distributing. It is also possible to play directly onto an instrument and the notator will display the music in note form on the screen.
- A **sound wave editor** is software which can be used to edit audio files, to create sound effects and to normalise, equalise, fade-in and fade-out music.
- **Digital radio and television services** have produced many channels, some of which are **pay-to-view services**. The user has to sign up to the service and agree to pay a fee every time he/she watches that channel. A similar idea is available in hotel rooms where standard television is free, but if the customer wants to watch a film he/she has to agree to add the cost of viewing to the hotel bill before that channel becomes available.
- **Teletext** services are usually news, sport or travel information which can be displayed as an addition to the television channel being watched. It is

possible to have the information displayed on-screen while the programme is being watched in the background, or with the information replacing the programme screen.

1.6 Shopping

- **Online shopping** – using a computer to order goods from a remote distributor – has revolutionised shopping. Millions of items are ordered online, particularly at Christmas. There are problems with shopping online as you cannot see or handle the goods prior to buying them, which is particularly difficult when buying clothes, and there are security problems involved with paying online with credit or debit cards. However, the convenience of being able to browse goods and order them at any time from the comfort of your own home and have them delivered to your door outweighs the disadvantages for most people.
- **E-commerce** is the use of the internet to transact business.
- **Electronic fund transfer (EFT)** transfers money between banks electronically. It can also occur in a shop when a purchaser pays using a debit card. The funds are transferred from the customer's bank to the shop's bank at the time of purchase. This is known as **electronic fund transfer at point of sale (EFTPOS)**. When **automatic teller machines (ATM)** are used to withdraw cash, the same principle applies.
- **Electronic points of sale (EPS)** are used by supermarkets linked to stock-control systems. Goods on sale in the supermarket have **barcodes** printed on them. The barcodes usually contain a unique serial number for the item, plus information such as the country of origin of the goods. A database contains all the information about the item with that particular serial number, such as who supplies it, its price and how many are in stock, and any special offers attached to the description of the item. When the barcode is read using a **laser scanner** or **hand-held barcode reader**, the code is looked up in the database and certain activities occur:
  - a sound is made to inform the checkout operator that the item has been scanned successfully
  - 1 is deducted from the number of items left in stock
  - the price of the item and a brief description is sent to the EPS to be printed on the till receipt and to be displayed on the LED display of the till
  - the price of the item is added to the total
  - the system will check if the **re-order level** has been reached
  - a check is made to see if any special offers have been made, such as 'two for the price of one'

If the item needs to be weighed, it is placed on a machine which sends the weight of the item to the computer together with the code of the item, which the checkout operator will enter using a **keypad**.

If the item has a barcode that cannot be read, perhaps because it is creased or damaged, then the checkout operator will key in the code manually. Keeping account of how much is in stock and informing the managers automatically when goods need reordering is known as **automatic stock**

control. Modern supermarkets have small or non-existent storage areas, usually just an unloading area. Nearly all the supermarket stock is on display on the shelves. It is important to have just enough stock to satisfy the customers' needs and not to overflow the shelves. This type of stock control is known as a **just-in-time** system.

- Some supermarkets have introduced **serve yourself tills** to allow customers to scan their own items and pay for them using cash or card without the need for an assistant. Several controls have to be in place to prevent the customer from stealing items or from sticking a bar code for something cheap (e.g. a tin of beans) onto something expensive (e.g. a bottle of whisky).

- Supermarkets issue **loyalty cards** to their customers, which benefit the supermarket as well as the customer. The customer usually benefits by getting goods or cash from points collected, and the supermarket gains by learning customers' shopping habits and targeting them appropriately with adverts. For instance, a customer's habit of purchasing dog food may imply he/she has a dog, so the supermarket can target the customer with special offers related to dogs. It would be a waste of their time to advertise dog products to customers who do not own dogs.

1.7 Marketing

- **Data mining** is the analysis of large quantities of data collected to find out information, such as the preferences of customers collected by a loyalty card system. Data mined in this way can often be worth huge amounts of money to companies.

- Marketing using **websites** will allow a company to reach a wide audience. A website costs very little to produce and can be updated regularly. Buying and selling online can take place and customers are able to carry out **price comparisons** online, either by exploring websites themselves or by using dedicated price comparison websites.

- As seen in Topic 4, spreadsheets **modelling** marketing situations can save time and money for companies.

1.8 Communication

- **Email** enables people to communicate easily if they have a computer linked to a network or internet. Email allows users to send a message with an attachment (which might be an image, sound or text file). A message can be sent to more than one person at once without any extra expense. It is possible to send copies to people or to reply by hitting a button. Groups of contacts can be set up and separate address books can be created, for instance one for business contacts and one for personal contacts. Since messages and attachments arrive in electronic format they can be incorporated into other electronic documents. Email is not secure but can be encrypted. Emails can often be **spam**, which are usually un-requested and unwanted advertising emails.

- **Voice mail services** are centralised telephone answering machines, but much more sophisticated than the old-fashioned answering machine. They can store messages in personalised mailboxes, answer more than one call at

once, store messages and deliver them at a later date, forward messages, and send messages to more than one other person.

● **File Transfer Protocol (FTP)** is used to control a file being transferred from one computer to another using the internet. A protocol is a standard set of rules which is used to make sure that data is properly transferred between devices.

● Other uses of the internet are **newsgroups**, which are message storage areas related to particular special interest subjects that users can subscribe to, **chat rooms** where like-minded people can meet virtually to discuss subjects of interest, and **online databases** where large quantities of information are stored, ranging from scientific information to genealogical data.

2 *Legal aspects of ICT*

As ICT becomes more involved in the everyday life of individuals, it is important that individuals and companies have as much protection from the consequences of ICT as possible. Laws are made by governments for a particular country, and by some larger organisations such as the European Union. The laws summarised in Table 7.1 are those Acts of Parliament created by the British government with jurisdiction in Great Britain. Other countries may have similar laws. You should try to find out more about each one and study them in greater detail.

Act	Purpose	Implications
Data Protection Act (1998)	To help protect people from the misuse of information that may be stored about them	Individuals have the right to see what is held about them on databases and to insist that it is accurate. Companies have to keep the data safe and only use it for the purpose for which it was collected.
Computer Misuse Act (1990)	To help protect the data held by companies from being stolen or misused by hackers	Unauthorised access to data is punishable by law.
Copyright, Designs and Patents Act (1988)	To make it illegal to copy software without the permission of the owner	It is a punishable offence to copy games and other items which should be paid for.
Regulation of Investigatory Powers Act (2000)	To make it illegal to intercept emails, phone calls, letters and other communications without permission	This is mostly to protect the individual from the state and means that groups such as the police cannot eavesdrop on conversations without special permission.
Electronic Communications Act (2000)	To set up a register of cryptographers, to help e-commerce and recognise digital signatures	Building confidence in e-commerce.

Act	Purpose	Implications
Freedom of Information Act (2000)	To make provision for the disclosure of information held by public authorities or by persons providing services for them and to amend the Data Protection Act 1998	An individual has a statutory right of access to information publicly available. The Act covers a wide range of public authorities, including local government, National Health Service bodies, schools and colleges, and the police.

Table 7.1 Acts of Parliament covering ICT

3 Combating ICT crime and protecting ICT systems

The government has passed a number of Acts of Parliament to make clear what is legal and illegal in relation to ICT. Individuals and organisations must take their own steps, within the framework of the law, to protect their own data and to make their systems secure. We must also protect ourselves against identity theft, which can happen if too much personal data is left unprotected. We should do this in the same way that a householder will try to protect their house, belongings and family – it is each individual's responsibility. Some of the methods used to keep our data, identity and systems secure include the following:

- Data should be kept under lock and key.
- Firewalls can help prevent unauthorised access from network traffic.
- Backups should be made so that if data is lost it can be recovered.
- Encryption can be used so that if data falls into wrong hands it cannot be understood.
- Biometric security, such as fingerprint or retina scans, can make sure the right person is accessing the data.
- Software patches and updates keep the software viable by repairing gaps in security that may be noticed over time and allow the user to keep one step ahead of the hackers.
- Anti-virus and anti-spyware software helps prevent a virus from attacking the computer and stops hackers accessing private details.
- Access rights can be granted that allow certain people specific rights to certain data.
- Auditing allows logs of activity to be kept so that the user knows who was where, when, and doing what.
- User IDs allow the computer to know who has what rights on the system (such as what files they have the right to access) and to allow the network manager to know which user is doing what on the system (such as which software is being used by that user).
- Passwords should be used, including letters and change of case. Passwords should be changed often and should not be related to personal details. Never tell anyone your password.

IDs tell the computer who the person is, and passwords prove the person is who they says they are.

4 : *Health and safety*

4.1 Health problems related to working with ICT

Table 7.2 sets out some common health problems related to working with ICT.

Problem	Description	Prevention
Carpal tunnel syndrome	Pains in the wrist from repetitive actions such as working for long hours on a keyboard.	Avoid repetitive actions – take frequent breaks.
Ulnar neuritis	Pains in the elbow from compressing the ulnar nerve caused by leaning on the elbow.	Use an adjustable chair, correct desk and wrist rests.
Deep vein thrombosis	A blood clot, often in the leg, caused by sitting still for a long time.	Use an adjustable chair, correctly positioned, and take exercise in breaks.
Eyesight defects	Sore, dry or tired eyes caused by looking at screens for long periods of time.	Use an adjustable monitor with brightness and contrast controls. Take regular breaks and have correct lighting in the room.
Fatigue	General tiredness or stress caused by repeating the same activity for long periods.	Take regular breaks and change activity from time to time. Drink plenty of water as working in air-conditioned areas can cause the body to lose moisture.
Repetitive strain injury	Pain in arms, hands, shoulders or back from incorrect posture at the computer and prolonged contact without a break.	Use an adjustable chair, foot rest, proper computer desk and ergonomic keyboard. Change activity from time to time, take regular breaks.
Backache	Pain in the back from poor posture at the computer.	Sit properly and use an adjustable chair which has been properly adjusted.
Stress	Fatigue, irritability and despair caused by long periods at the computer without a break.	Take frequent breaks, avoid repetitive activity, drink water, talk to colleagues between tasks.

Table 7.2 Health problems relating to ICT

4.2 Safety problems related to working with ICT

Table 7.3 sets out some common safety problems related to working with ICT.

Problem	Description	Prevention
Trailing wires	People could trip over the wires, pull equipment off shelves or electrocute themselves.	Wires should be cleared away and kept in 'cable tidies'.
Risk of fire and electrocution	Bare or worn wires or badly wired plugs can cause sparks or electrocution.	Plugs and wires should be inspected periodically. Wiring and fixing plugs should be carried out by a qualified person.
Unsecured equipment	Monitors and other equipment balanced precariously on shelves might fall, damaging people and equipment.	All equipment should be properly secured or mounted on strong secure surfaces.
Food	Food in keyboards can cause disease. Sticky fingers from eating while working can make equipment unsanitary.	Never eat in a proximity to a computer.
Drink	Spilled drink can cause damage to equipment and, in the worst case scenario, electrocution.	Never drink near a computer.
Proximity to water	Water and electricity cause electrocutions and damage to equipment.	Never have a source of water in a computer room. Fire extinguishers must be of the powder or carbon dioxide type.

Table 7.3 Safety problems relating to ICT

You will not find sprinklers in a computer room. Why?

Topic summary

Impact of ICT — advantages, disadvantages and consequences of developments in ICT for society, organisations and individuals.

Fields of development — transport, medicine, helping the disabled, education, entertainment, shopping, marketing, communication.

Legal aspects of ICT — Data Protection Act (1998), Computer Misuse Act (1990), Copyright, Designs and Patents Act (1988), Regulation of Investigatory Powers Act (2000), Electronic Communications Act (2000), Freedom of Information Act (2000).

Combating ICT crime — methods used to keep our data, identity and systems secure.

Health and safety — common problems related to working with ICT.

1 The systems cycle

When a computer system is built and put into operation it immediately starts to age. The process that occurs as a result of this is called the systems development life cycle (Figure 8.1). As a system ages, problems occur which need to be solved, and eventually these problems are so great that the system is no longer running efficiently. At this point, the cycle begins again with a new investigation and analysis.

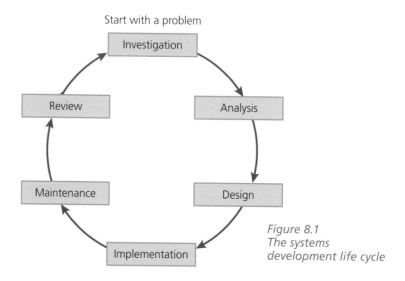

Figure 8.1
The systems development life cycle

Many high-profile ICT systems had to be scrapped because the expectations of the client were not fully understood by the analysts.

1.1 Definition of the problem

The problem must be understood by the client with the problem and the systems analysts charged with solving the problem. The nature of the problem must be agreed between the analysts and the client. This will probably take the form of an initial contract to undertake an investigation, followed by a **feasibility study**. The feasibility study will inform the client whether, in the opinion of the analysts, it is possible to solve the problem. A new system might be not feasible because:

- solving the problem is too expensive
- the hardware or software does not exist or cannot be produced
- there is no realistic solution to the problem (e.g. requiring anti-gravity devices)
- it would take too long to produce.

1.2 Investigation of the problem

Analysts are often viewed with suspicion and associated with job losses or loss of pay and status, as skilled workers are often replaced with machines.

In order to understand the existing system the analysts should undertake a detailed study of the company and how it operates at the moment, with particular attention to how the defined problem could be solved. There are several methods available to the analysts. They could **interview** the people who work in the company and with the problem and record the findings for later analysis. They might **observe** them at work – people are often unable to articulate accurately how they do something, or may exaggerate or lie about the time taken to do a task or about its complexity.

If there are a lot of employees to talk to, or the company has many branches across the country or the world, or the customers need to be included in the investigation, **questionnaires** could be sent out. **Meetings** could also be held to involve customers, shareholders or a wider audience. Analysts will **examine** the existing documents and records and note how the system inputs, outputs and records the data.

1.3 Analysis of the findings

The findings from the investigation need to be analysed and a set of proposals made as to how the problem is to be solved and what is to be included in the new system. This is summarised in a requirements specification.

The requirements specification

The requirements specification is a written document that clarifies for the client and the analyst what is being proposed for the new system. It includes:
- the customer requirements
- the functional requirements of the system – what it is expected to do
- details of the proposed performance of the system
- details of the proposed security of the system
- a timescale for completion of the system
- any major constraints

The requirements specification becomes the basis of the progress of the system. The system should be designed to meet the requirements and at the end of the process an evaluation is made as to whether the system meets the original requirements.

1.4 Design of the new system

Once the analysts have understood exactly what is needed by the new system and have seen how the present system works, they must design the system. To aid them they need:
- the requirements specification (agreed between the user and the analysts)
- a design specification (created by the analysts for use by the designers)
- the system specification (detailing what hardware and software is required in the new system)
- a test plan

The design specification

The design specification is drawn up from the requirements specification and informs the designers about what is needed. It should contain:
- the purpose of the system
- validation rules
- the inputs, outputs and processes
- the links between sections of the system
- data flow diagrams
- assumptions limitations and constraints
- data structures
- colours/fonts/sizes

The system specification

The systems specification includes:

- the hardware to be used
- the software it will be written with
- the people involved in the design of the system
- the way the system will be organised

The test plan

During the design phase of the system cycle, tests are devised to make sure that the system is working correctly. A test plan is created. This is often in the form of a table that shows:

- what is to be tested
- what **test data** is to be used
- what the outcome of the test is expected to be

When the system is built, it will be tested during the implementation stage to find out whether the test expectations have been met.

An example of the beginnings of a test plan are shown in Table 8.1.

Test	Test data	Expected outcome	Actual outcome
Customer first name input field	Jonathan	Name accepted and stored in customer table.	
Customer first name input field	12/3/79	Data rejected. Error message 'Please type first name only'.	

Table 8.1 Test plan for customer details input form

If the system is not tested properly there could be serious consequences. In 1992, the London Ambulance Service introduced a new ambulance dispatch service which had not been designed properly or tested rigorously. As a result, a number of deaths occurred that could have been avoided had the ambulances arrived on time. In 2004, a spokesman for the Child Support Agency admitted that its computer system would not work properly and had been badly tested. There are many other examples. You have probably run software yourself that has not worked properly, which presumably was not tested properly.

1.5 Implementation of the new system

Once the design has been finalised, it needs to be built and installed. This involves:

- obtaining the hardware
- obtaining or writing the software
- writing the documentation
- training personnel in the use of the new system
- discussing changes of working practice, redundancies, relocation etc. with employees

- testing the system with and without users to make sure that it meets the requirements decided at the outset
- installation of the system for the user, including transfer of data from the old system if necessary
- writing the documentation for the user and for the technicians who have to maintain the system

1.6 Evaluating the system

Evaluating the system involves a formal approach to see if the client agrees that the analysts have made a good job of creating and installing the new system and that work using the new system can begin.

At this point, the main job of the analysts is finished, though they will remain on call for possible hitches, bugs and general help as the system gets fully into action.

1.7 Reviews and maintenance

A regular pattern of reviews of the system performance is established and maintenance of the system will need to be carried out occasionally. This could be:
- adaptive maintenance
- perfective maintenance
- corrective maintenance

(The process of maintenance and review is covered in more detail in Topic 12.)

Working through the traditional systems cycle can be take too long for some projects – rapid application development (RAD) can be used to get to an end result more quickly. See below.

1.8 Repeating the cycle

Eventually, the system will become too patched up to function efficiently. Over time, the needs of the company and the customers may have changed and so major problems may arise which need solving. The analysts are called in and the cycle begins again.

1.9 Software development methodologies

In order to develop a new system it is often necessary to create new software or adapt existing software. It is rare that a solution can be found on sale and readily available. Sometimes a project can take so long to develop that the original requirements are no longer valid. For instance, in the late 1980s it was proposed that a new air traffic control system should be developed for England and Wales. It took so many years to develop that the original specifications were changed many times. The number of flights increased dramatically with the expanding of regional airports and the availability of cheap flights. The system was finally implemented in 2002, around 6 years late. At a final cost of over £600 million, the system far exceeded the original budget.

To help solve such inertia with large projects, analysts can use **rapid application development (RAD)**. RAD techniques enable the traditional systems cycle to be speeded up, though there have to be compromises. The developers can do a number of things to help speed up the development of the new system:

- **Use prototypes**. Prototyping is a method by which the designer first designs part of a system, e.g. a user interface. This is then tested by a user or group of users. Based on the comments of the user, the designer refines the original design, which can go back to the user for further evaluation. This process of design–refine–design can be repeated many times until the system is satisfactory. The process of repeating the design–refine–design loop is sometimes known as **iteration**.
- **Work in small teams**. Sometimes large groups of people can be unwieldy and a small team of individuals capable of carrying out a variety of tasks can be highly motivated and more flexible, bypassing the inherent inertia of a large team.
- **Time boxing** involves not waiting for one stage of the system life cycle to finish before beginning the next. As long as the version is working, refinements can come later.
- **Automated code generators** can be used to create software. By using computers to produce part of the program code, and whatever other new developments might be available, it is possible to speed up the process of developing the new system.

Advantages	Disadvantages
• Development is speeded up. • The time taken to delivery is shortened. • Users are involved extensively in the analysis and design stages, thus improving the quality of the finished product and getting it to match the initial requirements closely.	• Early versions may lack refinement. • Early versions may not have all the features requested in the requirements specification. • The final product may not be as scalable as a complete application. It will be 'fit for purpose' but will not have flexibility. • The client may be disappointed with early versions, though this is offset by the user involvement in the development.

Table 8.2 Advantages and disadvantages of RAD

2 *Project management*

In large teams there are certain well-defined roles. People with the particular skills to fulfil those roles will be recruited as team members. In small teams, one person may have more than one responsibility. The traditional team consists of the following:

- The **project manager** who oversees the running of the project and worries about **deadlines** (will the project be completed on time?) and **finances** (is the project staying within budget?). He/she makes sure that all the technical and user documentation is completed, and prepares reports on what still needs to be done.
- The **systems analyst** who examines the existing system and prepares the ground for the designer. He/she decides whether the system is suitable for upgrading or, if it is a new system, whether it is feasible to go ahead with the project.

- The **systems designer** who designs the inputs, processes and outputs of the system based on the findings of the analyst and to match the system requirements.
- The **programmer** and **tester** who produce the system according to the design and test it to make sure that the system does what it is supposed to do.

A systems analyst needs certain personal skills as well as an understanding of the techniques of analysing a system. Since he/she is working with people who may be suspicious of the reason the analyst is present, and who may be resentful at an implied disregard of a valued skill developed over many years, the analyst must be sensitive and uncritical. He/she should be introduced to the company where the work is to be carried out carefully. Initially, the analyst may confer with the managing director of the company, who can then introduce the analyst to the section heads. The section heads introduce the analyst to the members of the different departments in the company, emphasising that the new system should make the company more viable, up-to-date and efficient. In summary, the personal qualities needed by a systems analyst are :

- technical skills
- understanding of the problems
- good interpersonal relations
- administrative skills
- analytical skills

3 *Process modelling*

3.1 Critical path analysis (CPA)

Various tools have been developed to help the systems analyst plan the project so that it runs smoothly. **Critical path analysis (CPA)** is used to establish the shortest practical route through the construction of a system, bearing in mind that some parts of the task take longer than others and that some parts have to be completed before others. CPA helps answer the following questions:

- What are the tasks to be carried out?
- Where can parallel activity be performed?
- What is the shortest time in which the project can be completed?
- What resources are needed to execute the project?
- What is the sequence of activities, scheduling and timings involved?
- What are the task priorities?

A CPA chart could be created for one part of the system cycle. Figure 8.2 shows a chart for a system implementation.

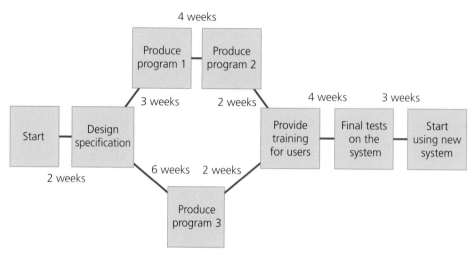

Figure 8.2 CPA chart for a system implementation

The chart shows that the critical path is the one running through program 1 and 2, since that part of the implementation takes a total of 9 weeks, whereas to produce program 3 and train the users only takes 8 weeks. The project itself will take a total of 2 + 3 + 4 + 2 + 4 + 3 = 18 weeks following the critical path. There is **slack time** available on the path through program 3.

3.2 PERT charts

Another way of representing the processes diagrammatically is using a **PERT chart**. PERT (programme evaluation and review technique) charts allow the analyst to plan the task using milestones represented by circles. Generally, the milestones are numbered in steps of ten so that others can be added later if necessary. The PERT chart in Figure 8.3 reproduces the information Figure 8.2.

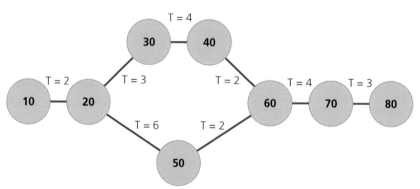

Figure 8.3 PERT chart for a system implementation

3.3 Gantt charts

Gantt charts are used to plot the possible progress of the project through time. Each activity is shown as a block of time. An example Gantt chart is shown in Figure 8.4.

	Week																	
	1	2	3	4	5	6	7	8	9	10	11	12	13	14	15	16	17	18
Task 10																		
Task 20																		
Task 30																		
Task 40																		
Task 50																		
Task 60																		
Task 70																		
Task 80																		

Figure 8.4 Gantt chart

Tasks are initially numbered in tens so that other tasks can be fitted in later if necessary.

3.4 Designers' tools

There are several tools useful to designers:
- entity relationship diagrams
- state transition diagrams
- data flow diagrams
- flowcharts
- structure diagrams

Entity relationship diagrams

When a database is being designed, the entities (tables) and attributes (fields) have to be defined. It is necessary to know the relationships between the entities. Entity relationship diagrams are discussed further in Topic 5.

State transition diagrams

These are used to describe every possible **state** of a single object and everything that changes the state of that object. These changes are known as **transitions**. They are useful for describing the behaviour of an object in every possible situation. Take the example of a milk-bottle filling machine. The milk bottle in the process of being filled can have the following states:
- empty
- being filled
- full
- capped
- broken

This could be represented using the following state transition diagram.

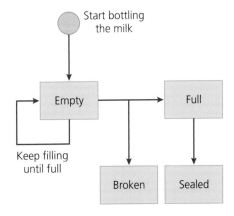

Figure 8.5

Data flow diagrams

Data flow diagrams are useful representations of the data input into a system, the processes the data goes through and the outputs from the system. The following symbols are used to create data flow diagrams.

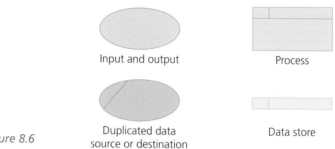

Figure 8.6

Flowcharts

Flowcharts allows a visual representation of the processes involved in a system. Symbols have been developed to represent processes and the symbols are connected by **flow lines** to indicate the flow of data through the system.

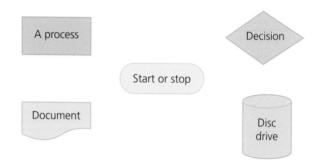

Figure 8.7

Structure diagrams

In a structure diagram the system is described as a number of levels. Each level describes the whole design, but the detail increases as the levels increase. This is sometimes called top-down design.

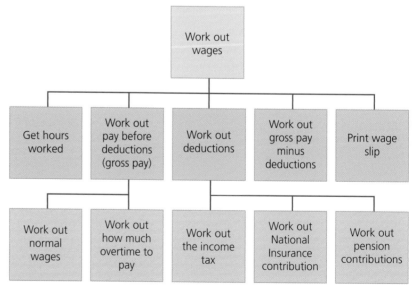

Figure 8.8

Topic summary

The systems cycle — investigation, analysis, design, implementation, maintenance, review.

Investigation — interview, observation, questionnaires, meetings, examination of documents.

Analysis — the requirements specification.

Design — design specification, system specification, test plan.

Implementation — building and installing the system.

Maintenance and review — regular pattern of review and adaptive, perfective and corrective maintenance.

Software development methodologies — using rapid application development (RAD).

Project management — project manager, systems analyst, systems designer, programmer and tester.

Process modelling — critical path analysis (CPA), PERT charts, Gantt charts, designers' tools.

1 Processing systems

A **processing system** is one that operates on the data input in a particular way. Each system needs software known as an **operating system** to make it function. There are several types of processing systems used for a variety of tasks, each with its own operating system.

A **single-user system** is one such as a home computer or a laptop, not connected to any other computers. It is possible to run several programs at once (see multi-tasking system).

A **multi-user** or **multi-access system** is one in which a single computer is connected to a number of terminals but each user thinks that he/she has control of the computer. In other words, a number of users can use the same computer at the same time. This is achieved by each user being given a brief slice of processing time so often that they do not notice the time delay between one slice of time and the next. At the end of a normal working day the computer can be used to run a batch process (see below) by changing the operating system programs.

A **multi-tasking system** allows several applications to run simultaneously. This means that a user can have a number of programs running at the same time, for instance word-processing software, a web browser and an email package. This is useful if the user wants to cut and paste between applications. More importantly, with a multi-tasking system many programs run in the background (e.g. operating system), looking after the computer (e.g. anti-virus software) and allowing peripheral devices (e.g. printers) to be used without the user being aware of all the activity going on in the processor.

In **batch processing**, data is collected (batched) before the processing begins. The system can be run at times of least demand, such as at night when most of the staff have gone home. Once the work has started there is little user interaction with the system, as all the inputs have been collected beforehand. This is useful for tasks such as running a company payroll at the end of a month or producing personalised mailings to customers.

Interactive processing implies direct user interaction during the processing. The system responds immediately to the inputs from the user. This processing method is useful for dialogue, such as booking an airline ticket, using a customer-operated checkout at a supermarket, or getting a balance from an ATM.

In **transaction processing**, an individual item of processing, such as a booking or completing an order, is processed before the next order or booking is undertaken. Moving money from one account to another in the same bank a transaction process.

In **real-time processing**, the inputs immediately affect the outputs. For instance, modern cars use real-time electronics processing to communicate between the brake pedal and the brakes and the steering wheel and the wheels. Another example is when you book a holiday. Once you have booked a particular holiday no one else can have exactly the same one. If this was not the case, planes would be overbooked and several families might end up in the same hotel room.

Distributed processing is sharing out tasks between processors that are attached to the same network. This can speed up complex tasks, particularly those with a large amount of repetitive 'number crunching'.

> Response time is the time taken from the end of the input to the beginning of the output.

Processing systems	Response time	User interface
Batch	Could be long – up to a week or even a month	The interface is used by experts and so it can be a complex task to enter batch processing instructions
Interactive	Straight away	On-screen dialogue, forms, menus etc.
Transaction	Within a few seconds, depending on the system used	Probably an online booking form or other type of form-based interface
Real-time	Immediate	Usually hard-wired and used in process control, such as central heating, and consumer goods, such as video cameras

Table 9.1 Types of processing systems

2 The human–computer interface

2.1 Design characteristics

A **human–computer interface (HCI)** defines the communication between human and machine. The way in which this is enabled and the care with which the method is designed leads to the success or failure of the system. Many factors have to be taken into account. These include:

- **The use of colour**
  - Contrasting use of colour can highlight important functions.
  - Colours should be used sparingly so the screen does not become confusing.
  - Text should stand out clearly from the background – green text on green backgrounds is not a good idea.
  - Some colours have traditional meanings – green = OK, red = careful!
- **Layout**
  - The Western eye reads from left to right, so put important information at the top left.
  - Keep information in a logical order.
  - If actions are necessary then make sure that buttons and other action points are clearly seen and labelled.
- **Quantity of information on screen**
  - Don't present too much information at once – short-term memory will store little from a casual read through.
  - Instructions should not be repeated unnecessarily.

- Make some key words into links so users can follow the link if they need that information expanded.
- Don't highlight too much information, or it will cease to be special and will be ignored.

● **Size of font**
  - This should be appropriate to the task – young children need simple, large fonts; people at work may need more information in a smaller space.
  - Visually impaired people may need to adjust the size of the text to suit themselves.

● **Complexity of language**
  Bear in mind the user when putting instructions or information on the screen – a technician would need different instructions for how to install a program from an elderly person with no ICT background.

● **Type of controls**
  These should be appropriate to the task, such as:
  - buttons to run a specific action or to jump to another area of the screen
  - hyperlinks to jump to another document or elsewhere on the screen
  - drop-down boxes to limit choice
  - check boxes to allow a number of choices
  - radio buttons to limit choice to one option from a list

2.2 Styles of interface

Choose whether to have a menu driven, command line, natural language or graphic user interface. The advantages and disadvantages of each of these methods are reviewed in Topic 2.

2.3 Dialogue

A dialogue is a two-way flow of information and instructions between two systems. These systems might be human or computer. The dialogue can be as simple as that between a central heating thermostat and a processor, or as complex as the interaction taking place in a virtual reality game.

Dialogue can be between:
- human and human
- computer and human
- human and computer
- computer and computer

Dialogue between human and human involves the use of such things as body language, gesture, speech, touch and writing as outputs, and natural senses such as the sense of sight, hearing etc. Humans have evolved rules or **protocols** to govern the way in which our dialogue takes place. For a computer to be able to communicate with another computer, rules must be established. Because of the analogy between human–human interaction, these are also called protocols. It is not within the remit of A-level ICT to know particular details about computer transmission protocols, but you are probably familiar with some computer–computer protocols, such as:

A protocol is a set of rules which dictates the format of communications.

- **Transmission Control Protocol (TCP)** – this is sometimes linked with the Internet Protocol (IC) to give TCP/IP.
- **Simple Mail Transfer Protocol (SMTP)** – this is the standard for email transmissions on the internet.
- **Hypertext Transfer Protocol (HTTP)** – this can be seen in most web addresses such as http://www.philipallan.co.uk.

For humans to have a dialogue with a computer, methods of input, output and protocols must be developed. Some of these are summarised in Table 9.2.

Dialogue	Methods
Between computer and person — using screens, printers, speakers etc. Between person and computer – using keyboard, mouse, microphone etc.	• Command line interfaces • Menus and submenus/graphical user interfaces • Natural language using speech or writing • Forms
Between computer and computer – using wires, microwaves, infra-red etc.	Protocols such as: • TCP/IP • SMTP • http

Table 9.2 Methods of dialogue

2.4 Design requirements

It is important to take the user into account when designing the interface. There may be differences in design based on the fact that the user is:
- young or old
- experienced or inexperienced
- a non-native English speaker
- unable to see or hear, or use a keyboard

Equally, the environment for the use of the interface is important. Will it be used in:
- wet or dirty conditions (such as in a greenhouse)?
- hot or exposed sunny positions (such as an ATM on a sunny street)?
- hostile conditions (such as near a furnace or inside a volcano)?

An interface must be capable of being used:
- safely, such as entering instructions in a chemical plant
- effectively, such as using a mobile phone or recording a television programme
- efficiently, such as withdrawing money from an ATM
- enjoyably, such as when playing a computer game or buying an item online

2.5 The mental model

Every user approaching an interface will have an idea of how it will work. This is known as a **mental model**.

'As a last resort, read the manual' is an old joke with a lot of truth in it.

Look up 'interface hall of shame' on the internet to see traps and pitfalls of bad interface design.

Card, Moran and Newell published a book in 1983 called *The Psychology of Human–Computer Interaction*, in which they proposed the concept of 'mental models'. The concept has had a huge impact on the study of HCI.

Most people will expect to be able to operate a system by intuition or trial and error, and many experience rapid success in the early stages of trying a new system, which reinforces the belief that a new system can be operated without instructions. People get bored or disheartened quickly if they cannot make progress. If these people are a business's employees or your customers, poor interfaces could have serious consequences. It is therefore important to construct an HCI that closely matches the user's mental model. Careful attention to the design will lead to an increased speed of learning for users, more confidence for a beginner and an easy-to-use interface for everyone.

It has been discovered, through observation and experiment, that a potential user's **perception**, **attention**, **memory** and **learning** should be taken into account when designing an interface (see Table 9.3).

2.6 The model human processor

This is a user interface design tool developed by Card, Moran and Newell.

The 'model human processor' draws an analogy between the processing and storage of a computer with the perceptual, cognitive, motor and memory activities of a human. A visual or audible stimulus is captured (attention drawn to box on screen). The physical attributes of the stimulus are decoded (human interprets the response needed). A motor response based on past experience and the current situation is initiated (clicks a mouse). Figure 9.1 shows these activities.

Activities of a human related to a computer
- **Perceptual** – we receive information through our senses = our input devices:
  - sight
  - hearing
  - touch
  - taste
  - smell
- **Cognitive** – we think about things and work them out = our processing unit:
  - brain
  - knowledge
  - experience
- **Motor** – we act on our knowledge = our output devices:
  - limbs
  - speech
  - fingers
- **Memory** – we retain information for future use = our internal memory (RAM and ROM):
  - long-term memory
  - short-term memory.

RAM stands for random access memory. RAM computer chips act as a read/write memory in the computer. ROM stands for read only memory. ROM computer chips act as a memory but cannot be rewritten.

Attribute	Description and advice
Perception	• Perception is the input to the user via sight and sound. • The user has preconceived ideas such as green = go and red = stop. • Certain images and sounds are perceived as happy or sad. • Images, text and sounds must be clear, suitable for the purpose and straightforward. • A user who 'perceives' a screen as difficult to use will lose heart.
Attention	• The user has a limited attention span. • Attention can be maintained by the consistent use of colour and layout – don't wear the user out with an overload of information and clutter. • Clearly labelled screens with salient points made obvious will hold the attention of the user. • The use of logical menus and sub-menus for progress through the screens will also hold users' attention. • Use of flashing, inverse video, pop-up messages and sounds can draw attention to something.

Memory	• The short-term memory (less than 30 seconds) involves remembering something briefly, such as what was at the top of the page before scrolling to the bottom.
	• The screen should be uncluttered so that there is not too much to absorb and remember.
	• The user may use the screens infrequently, so they should be designed so that he/she will find the general layout and navigation methods familiar.
	• Long-term memory (lasting for longer than 30 seconds) stores data for future reference. A certain pattern of repeated events will 'stick in the mind', such as:
	  – choose goods
	  – click on shopping basket
	  – click 'pay by card'
	  – receive email confirmation
	  – receive goods
	• Page layouts should remain consistent to draw on the memory of previous screens and reinforce that memory to make the user more efficient and confident using the screens.

Learning	• The user may not be trained to use this interface, so the amount of learning needed must be minimal. • The use of the interface must be intuitive so that the majority of the moves the user makes come naturally. • The user needs to feel confident so that new skills necessary for using the interface can be learned in small amounts.

Table 9.3 Attributes to consider when designing an interface

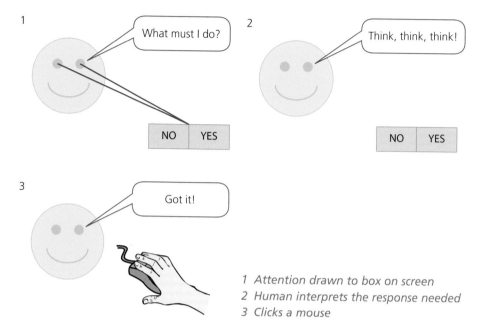

Figure 9.1 The model human processor

1 Attention drawn to box on screen
2 Human interprets the response needed
3 Clicks a mouse

Topic summary

Processing systems — single user, multi-user/multi-access and multi-tasking systems; batch, interactive, transaction, real-time and distributed processing.

The human–computer interface — design characteristics, design requirements, the mental model, the model human processor.

1 Networks

A stand-alone computer is of limited use. When computers are linked to form a network it becomes possible to carry out other tasks, such as communication and sharing of files. The advantages of networking computers can be summarised as follows:

- Communication between computers becomes possible, e.g. email.
- Sharing of hardware reduces costs. For example, one office can share a printer rather than having a printer for every computer.
- Data can be shared between computers. For example, there can be rapid access to a shared database. All those connected to the network can simultaneously receive updates of prices or a change of a customer's address.
- It becomes possible to monitor the traffic on the network and find out what every user is doing. Logs can be kept of how often particular packages are used, which has implications for site licenses.
- Security can be organised from a central point, meaning that traffic in and out of the network can be checked for viruses.
- It is easier to back up data from one central point than to back up each machine separately.

There are some disadvantages to networks:

- They are harder to keep secure.
- They may become slow with heavy use.
- If the network fails, shared resources may be unavailable and a business could suffer from not being able to carry out daily routines.

1.1 LANs and WANs

A network can be defined as a **local area network (LAN)**, a **wide area network (WAN)**, a **virtual local area network (VLAN)** or a **virtual private network (VPN)**.

LAN	WAN	VLAN	VPN
Covers a defined area, usually on one building or site.	Covers a wide geographical area.	Usually a virtual (logical) part of a LAN.	Usually uses a WAN.
Has direct connections between the computers and probably uses cables or wireless.	Computers are usually linked by using the infrastructure of the public communications system (e.g. telephone lines).	Creation is purely by software, as the links already exist.	Remote stations connect to a server using the internet.
The communication media is owned by the owners of the LAN.	The network is linked by communications methods owned by third parties.	Different members of a pre-defined group are able to use part of a network without being aware of the parts to which they have no access.	Security is ensured by using procedures such as encrypting the originators' and receivers' addresses.
		Several different VLANs can exist within one physical configuration.	Data is sent encrypted for additional security.

Table 10.1 Network characteristics

1.2 LAN topologies

Traditionally, LANs are connected in three main arrangements or **topologies**. These are **bus**, **ring** and **star**. Although they are a simplification of most modern network systems, these topologies show how computers can be joined to form LANs.

Two typical bus networks are shown in Figure 10.1. In diagram A, the bus is a cable going into and out of the network connections of each device. Diagram B shows a spur arrangement, where each device is connected to the main cable or bus by a short cable known as a **spur**.

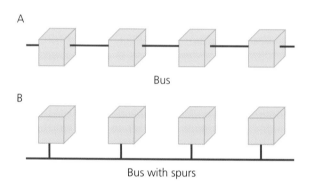

Figure 10.1

Figure 10.2 shows similar arrangements for a ring arrangement.

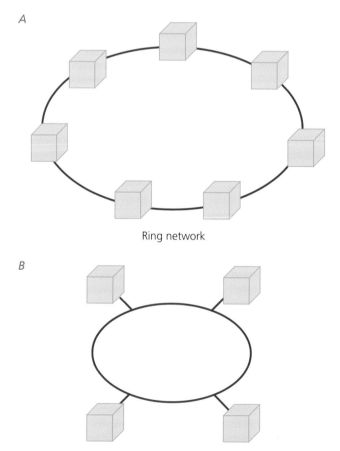

Figure 10.2   Ring network with spurs

Figure 10.3 is a star arrangement.

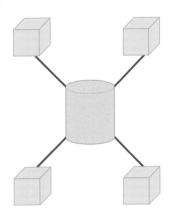

Figure 10.3

Note that in all the arrangements the devices do not all have to be computers, they could be disc drives, printers, scanners, photocopiers etc.

1.3 Client–server and peer-to-peer networks

A **client–server network** is organised around one or more servers to provide shared resources. The server also provides security for the network.

Peer-to-peer networks are a simple way of sharing resources by linking all the computers so that they can communicate.

	Advantages	Disadvantages
Client–server network	• Security for the network is provided from one place. • Allows sharing of software and data from one location. • Easier to back up shared data and other software as it is all held on the server. • Allows sharing of hardware resources without relying on other computers on the net.	• If the server fails, the network fails. • Requires a network administrator to operate successfully. • Can be an expensive option as the administrator needs to be employed and the accommodation for the server may need security and air conditioning.
Peer-to-peer network	• Simple to manage. • Relatively cheap to set up. • Does not require central management or much technical knowledge. • Resources can be shared from other stations on the network.	• Security is poor as each station has equal status. • As data is not centrally controlled, data duplication can take place. • If the computer acting as the printer server breaks down, no one can print. • Each computer must be backed up individually.

Table 10.2 Advantages and disadvantages of client–server and peer-to-peer networks

2 Internet and intranets

The **internet** is a network of computers across the world using existing telecommunications such as telephone lines and satellite links. It allows the sharing of unlimited data and resources, and allows such activities as messaging, shopping, banking, teaching and advertising to take place online. The coverage is worldwide and is generally unrestricted by governments or local conditions.

An **intranet** is a network providing similar services to the internet but within (for instance) one company or school. It is generally restricted to those who are part of a pre-defined group. An **extranet** is part of an intranet that is able to be accessed by the public using the internet.

The **World Wide Web** is the collection of multimedia information or resources available on the internet.

3 Communicating data

3.1 Bandwidth

Bandwidth is the measure of capacity of a communication channel such as a wire. It is measured in bits per second – how many bits (binary digits) can be transmitted along the line in 1 second. A high bit transmission rate is known as **broadband**.

Bandwidth can also be defined as the frequency range that it can handle. To be classified as broadband it must have a frequency range of more than 3KHz, though most modern broadband systems have a much greater range.

When data is sent over a network it is sent in **packets** of 0s and 1s. A simple message written at the keyboard is translated by the computer into a relatively small number of binary digits. A picture or video can be made of a huge number of bits. If the bandwidth is too small it will take a long time for the data to arrive, because only a small number of bits can be transmitted at once. As the bandwidth is increased, more bits can be transmitted. Note that a higher bandwidth does not mean the data travels faster. Imagine a single lane road with a lorry driving along it carrying a certain amount of goods and travelling at a fixed speed. Now imagine widening the road so that many lorries, all travelling at the same speed and carrying identical loads, are travelling side by side. No goods will arrive at the destination faster, but the amount of goods arriving is increased. So for large files, such as pictures or videos, broadband is useful. By delivering a lot of bits at a time and by using **buffering**, the video will run smoothly.

A standard broadband connection is known as **asymmetric digital subscriber line (ADSL)**. The distinguishing characteristic of ADSL is that it is **asymmetric** – the volume of data flow is greater in one direction than the other. This is useful for connecting to the internet as it can use the higher speed direction for downloading rather than uploading, which is of value for most users.

> A bit is a 0 or a 1. All digital data is transferred in 0s and 1s.

> Buffering is when the computer continuously collects the data as it arrives and stores it in a temporary holding area known as a buffer so that it can be released to the screen and speakers in a steady stream.

3.2 Communication media

Different types of communication media have different characteristics, e.g. some are not able to cope with high bandwidths, and some are not suitable for all locations. In addition, the distance between clients, the level of security needed and the cost of the connection must be taken into account when choosing the media.

The characteristics of a number of different media are shown in Table 10.3.

Media type	Characteristics	Advantages and disadvantages
Cables	Usually made of copper, the cables consist of pairs of wires twisted together to give protection against electrical interference. Cat5 unshielded twisted pair (UTP) cabling systems are the most common. Cat5 is generally used for ethernet networks running at 10 to 100 megabits per second.	+ High electrical conductivity of copper. + Ease of connecting. − Prone to electrical surges such as those caused by lightning strikes. − Long cables lose the strength of the signal. − Can only carry limited bandwidth.
Optical Fibre optics	Made from fine glass fibres. Transmit data in the form of light.	+ No electrical interference is possible. + No corrosion and no heat, sparks or electrical voltages are generated, so this media is very safe and reliable. + Very high bandwidths are possible, allowing data to be transmitted at hundreds of megabits per second. + Cables can be up to 5 km long before repeaters are needed to boost the signal. − Higher cost to install and more specialist knowledge is needed. − Transmission equipment is more expensive. − Fibres cannot carry power.
Infrared	Used in remote keyboards, mice, control units for televisions etc.	+ not subject to radio electrical interference − An uninterrupted line of sight between the sending and receiving devices is needed. − Sunlight may interfere with the signal.
Laser	Laser (light amplification by stimulated emission of radiation) light is different from normal light in that it has a highly focused beam with a narrow range of wavelengths. This means that it can travel long distances without dispersing.	+ Can link buildings as far apart as 4 km, at data speeds up to 1.5Gbps. + Suitable for LANs on split sites. + Direct beam, so very secure. − Prone to interference if anything interrupts the beam.
Wireless Radio waves	Radio waves are electromagnetic waves with relatively long wavelengths, e.g. waves from a few centimetres in length (FM radio) to hundreds of meters in length (AM radio).	+ Useful for sites that are difficult to wire up. + Useful for people needing communications with portable devices such as laptops. − Needs a transmitter. If the network is large there may need to be several transmitters. − Prone to electrical interference. − Not as secure as wired systems.

Media type	Characteristics	Advantages and disadvantages
Microwaves	Microwaves use transmitting and receiving dishes, often on towers to give further coverage. Used as part of the public telephone system. Signals are beamed from dish to dish across the country.	+ More secure than some systems because the signals are sent in a tight beam directly to the destination. + Useful for transmitting data between company sites in different parts of a city. – A clear line of sight is necessary.
Satellite links	A narrow signal beam is sent to the satellite from a ground station. The satellite directs the beam down to a receiver in another place.	+ Useful for long-distance communications, such as between countries. – Difficult to repair satellites if anything goes wrong.
Bluetooth®	An industrial specification for wireless personal area networks. Allows devices such as computers, PDAs, mobile phones, printers, cameras etc. to communicate wirelessly.	+ Normally has a range of up to 10 m, but can be boosted to 100 m. + Eliminates the difficulty of transferring data from one device to another. Printing from a PDA or mobile phone becomes easier. – Can be intercepted by any device within range, so not always secure.

Table 10.3 Characteristics of different media

3.3 Network components

Some of the common components that are used in creating networks of computers are shown in Table 10.4.

When a switch filters a packet of data it checks the packet against a set of 'rules' and discards the packet if it does not conform to those rules.

Network component	Role and use
Hub	A connection point between cables in a network. Managed hubs have extra features, such as monitoring traffic between them. A hub contains a number of ports. When a packet arrives at one port, it is copied to the other ports so that all segments of the LAN can see all packets. Some intelligent hubs can be used by the administrator to monitor network traffic.
Switch	A device that **filters** and forwards packets between segments of the LAN. A switch is more intelligent than a hub. Switches look at the data packets as they are received and forward the packet to the appropriate destination device. By delivering a message only to the device it was intended for, a switch offers better performance than a hub by conserving network bandwidth.
Wireless access point	A device on the network which acts as a hub for wireless access to the network.
Network interface card (NIC)	A piece of computer hardware that allows devices to connect to a wired network. Generally installed into a slot in the computer or peripheral.

Wireless network interface card	A piece of computer hardware that allows devices to connect to a wireless network.
Router	A router forwards data packets along a network. Routers are generally located at gateways (where two networks connect). They determine the best path for forwarding the packets, and they communicate with other routers to configure the best route between any two hosts.
Gateway	A system to allow a LAN to connect with a WAN such as the internet.
Repeater	A device that receives a signal and boosts it along the next leg of its journey. A series of repeaters may be used if the cables are very long. A repeater cleans up a signal by removing unwanted **noise**.
Bridge	A bridge connects a LAN to another LAN that uses the same protocol. A bridge takes each message on a LAN and sends it to the same LAN or forwards it to the other LAN. Bridges develop a **learning table** so that they can remember the destination of messages to make the process more efficient.

Table 10.4 Network components

Noise in networks is what we would call crackle or interference in a radio transmission. It can be caused by other electrical equipment nearby or by electrical activity in the weather, such as lightning.

When a message is sent out by a device on a network, the messages are sent to every address on the network system. Only the intended destination device will accept the message. A bridge is required because there will be more than one LAN on the system.

Server

A server can be considered as a computer, linked to the network, that runs **server software**. This computer generally is more powerful than other computers on the network because it processes data from all across the network and provide services for all network stations. Because all users rely on it to store data and provide applications, it must never fail. It will probably have built-in hubs or be connected to a set of hubs. It will have a set of hard drives so that all data is written identically to more than one drive. If one fails the other will take over the work while the first is repaired. This system is known as **redundant arrays of inexpensive discs (RAID)**. There will also be an **uninterrupted power supply (UPS)** in case of power failure.

There are a number of types of server, though in many cases one computer will provide more than one of the services. The **file server** provides the central disc storage and holds the user accounts and password details. Access rights, supplied by the network administrator, are stored here. An **applications server** will hold software such as word processors and databases that can be accessed by any station on the network. When a user wishes to use such a package it is temporarily copied to their machine across the network. This makes monitoring the use of applications easier for site licence purposes and makes updating the software more efficient since it only has to be updated on one computer.

A **mail server** manages the email for a network. It stores email until a user logs on to the network, and then forwards messages. It can act as a filter to screen out junk mail. The **print server** manages the print queues and printers attached to the network, while the **backup server**, a separate computer or disc system, such as RAID, copies all essential data and software in case the main server stops working.

A **proxy server** is an application that usually 'stands guard' at the point where a LAN meets the internet to isolate the WAN from the LAN. It stops unauthorised access to the LAN by external users and filters what can be accessed from outside for the internal users. It usually is associated with a firewall.

4 Communication applications

Networks provide a number of communication applications by using telecommunications systems and the internet.

4.1 Fax

Fax, an abbreviation for facsimile, allows copies of paper-based documents to be sent to another part of the network. A fax machine essentially consists of a scanner and printer linked to a telephone system. The document to be copied is scanned and the digitised version is sent across the telephone system to a receiving fax machine, where it is printed. Computer software has been developed to allow computers to act as fax machines, with the advantage that the documents can be stored electronically and not printed unless necessary. Fax machines become inefficient if the paper or ink runs out. They are also prone to **spam**, as firms can send adverts to any fax machine but the recipient has to bear the costs of printing the document. Faxed documents are not necessarily secure, as anyone who is by the machine when a document arrives can read it. There is also no guarantee that the document has arrived at the correct machine if the fax number was dialled incorrectly.

4.2 Email

Electronic mail (email) is a system which allows users to send messages to one another. Each user has a mailbox held on the computer or a server. **Webmail** may be held on the internet host's server. Email makes it possible to:
- send/receive messages to/from an individual
- send/receive messages to/from a group of users
- send a reply to a message
- delete messages no longer required
- store messages in folders
- compose draft messages
- send and receive attachments
- keep an address book.

Compared with normal mail, email has advantages and disadvantages.

Advantages:

- Mail can be read and replies made without using paper.
- Messages can be received almost immediately after they are sent if the user is logged on.
- It is effectively free once the equipment has been purchased and the internet provider has been paid.
- It is convenient as all mail can be sent without leaving the computer.

Disadvantages:

- Email can only be sent to people who possess the necessary hardware and software.
- The mail is only read when a user logs on.
- Once on an email system, the user is often bombarded with spam and junk mail and **phishing** emails.

Phishing is an attempt to gather information such as passwords, bank account details and other personal information by inducing email users to part with them. Bogus websites are often used.

4.3 Bulletin (discussion) boards

A bulletin board is like a notice board where information can be displayed electronically. It could be displayed automatically when someone logs on to a network, or it might be reached following a short-cut from a desktop display. It is possible for messages, comments etc. to be left on the board so that anyone logging on can read all the messages left there.

4.4 Tele/video-conferencing

This is the use of communications links to conduct meetings between people who are geographically separated. The links include voice and pictures. To provide this service, hardware such as a webcam and a microphone are needed, as well as an appropriate room and software to manage the conference. A broadband connection is needed. There are a number of advantages, such as not having to travel to the meeting, thereby saving money on hotels and fares. Participants will spend less time away from their work, meaning that they can spend more time with their customers. There is less chance of making bad decisions owing to tiredness from travelling. There is the potential to hold meetings more often because no time is wasted in travelling between venues. New products and new initiatives are better explained using voice and pictures than when sending a memo.

4.5 Internet relay chat (IRC)

IRC is a method of communicating in groups or individually using networks and the internet. It is possible to join **forums** or **online discussion groups** and have real-time chat with the other members. There are thousands of **chat rooms** where a huge range of discussions can take place, on topics ranging from aardvarks to zebras, from politics to fashion. If you cannot find a chat group which covers your favourite topic, you can form one of your own and invite others to join in.

4.6 Mobile phones

Mobile phones have become popular over the last 10 years. From their origins as large, brick-like objects, they have developed into small sophisticated devices which can make and receive phone calls, take photos, play music, act as a PDA, connect to the internet, and send and receive emails and messages called **texts**. Coverage is worldwide – it is possible to be sat on a beach in Australia while talking to someone in England. It is also possible to use a mobile phone to control devices such as central heating and lights, so you can 'phone home' and give and receive messages from the house control system.

A mobile phone network operates in two ways: the land-based **cellular network** and the global **satellite network**.

Cellular network

The area to be covered by a phone provider is broken up into a series of **cells**. Each cell has a base station at the centre and probably a mast for broadcasting and picking up signals. As a phone nears the edge of one cell, the signal gradually becomes weaker. Before the phone loses the signal it starts to pick up signals from an adjacent cell. When a mobile phone is switched on, it searches for the strongest signal of those available and automatically logs on to that base station. Because each base station has an identification, it is possible to know roughly where a person is when they are making a mobile phone call. As this information is recorded for billing purposes, it is often used in legal cases where a person's whereabouts at a particular time has to be confirmed. The mobile phone network is linked to the standard telephone system, so calls can be made to and from landlines.

The advantages of using a cellular system are:
- It is reasonably cheap for local calls.
- Users can make or receive calls anywhere covered by the network.
- Many cellular phones can also take photos.

The disadvantages are:
- Users cannot make a phone call if they are out of range of a base station.
- Some people believe that living near a base station or using a mobile phone for a long time has negative health implications, though there is no convincing evidence that this is true.
- Reception can be lost inside buildings or tunnels.
- Calls can be expensive.

Satellite mobile phones

With this system, the phone signals are sent to satellites in **geo-stationary orbit** or to **low earth orbit (LEO)** satellites which orbit the Earth, flying fast and low. Geostationary means that the satellite stays over the same position on Earth all the time. The satellite is set in orbit so that its speed is such that it appears to be stationary in the sky. The satellites orbit at a great altitude, about 22,000 miles above the surface of the Earth. A sufficient number of satellites are in orbit so that there is usually one within range everywhere on the surface of the Earth.

LEO satellites move so fast (orbiting the Earth in just over 1 hour) that if a building or mountain is in the way it is only necessary to wait a few minutes for another one to pass by, allowing the call to be made.

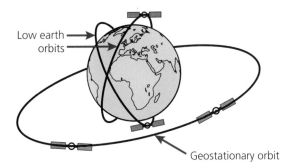

Figure 10.4 Satellite orbits
Satellites can be stationary relative to a point on the Earth – geostationary – or orbit the Earth at a lower altitude

Satellite phones have bulky aerials or can be linked to portable satellite dishes. They are large compared with the modern cell phone. There must be direct line of sight between the phone and the satellite, so if a mountain or building gets in the way the user must get higher to avoid the obstacles.

The main advantage of satellite phones over cell phones is that it is possible to make a call from anywhere on Earth. The disadvantages are:
- There is a delay in the signal because of the distances involved.
- Satellite phones are much more expensive than cell phones to buy and the system is much more expensive to set up (launching satellites). It is also more expensive to make the calls.
- Lack of sight of a satellite may delay the making of the call.

The implications of being able to communicate from anywhere in the world using mobile technology are significant. Particularly in times of crisis, international rescue teams and troops can communicate with their home countries, reporting on conditions and asking for equipment and personnel. News reporters can send live reports from the remotest parts of the Earth, keeping us up to date on the latest happenings. This may mean that news reaches us so quickly that we react too fast to that news – an hour later, more news will change the way we think about the event.

4.7 Satellites

As well as being used for making telephone calls, satellites have a number of other uses.

Global positioning
A **global positioning system (GPS)** is a receiver that can pick up radio signals from satellites orbiting the Earth. There are 27 satellites in the GPS system, of which 24 are operational and three are spares. At any given time, four are in range of a GPS receiver. Each satellite transmits a signal at exactly the same time. The receiver can time how long each signal takes to arrive and thus

calculate the distance from the satellite. With signals from three satellites the receiver can pinpoint its position on the surface of the Earth, and with a fourth can also work out its altitude. GPS systems need a line of sight to function, so will not work well in woods and buildings. When combined with built-in maps, the device can display the user's position on a screen and give names of roads and towns. With software added, the GPS can tell the user:

- how far he/she has gone since starting the journey
- the length of time he/she has been travelling
- his/her current speed
- his/her average speed
- a line on the map to show where he/she has been
- an estimated time of arrival if the destination is known

The advantages of using satellites for GPS systems is that, once launched, little will interfere with them. They broadcast all over the world, so with the correct receiving equipment anyone, anywhere, can use the system. GPS allows ocean-going ships to work out their position and thereby avoid rocks and hazards, and orienteering leisure groups to know where they are. A popular use is in cars – drivers can safely find a route without having to concentrate on maps, as the system will speak the directions out loud.

The Disadvantage of using satellites is that they are very difficult to repair if they malfunction. It is also expensive to set up the system initially.

Weather monitoring and forecasting

Weather forecasting involves many readings from around the world taken by direct observation, weather balloons, aircraft, remote weather stations and satellites. The satellites gather data on visible or infrared radiation, moisture in the atmosphere, solar radiation and temperature, which are sent to be processed into the pictures we are familiar with from weather forecasts. One simple way of forecasting the weather is to look at a sequence of images taken over time to form a short film, from which the pattern of cloud movement can be determined. Modern weather forecasting takes data from thousands of sources, including satellites, and uses powerful computers to calculate the pressures, temperatures, wind speed and direction etc.

The advantages of using satellites is that they can work continuously, regardless of the weather on Earth. They are much more reliable than human beings taking similar measurements (even if that was possible). They are expensive to launch, however, and difficult to repair if they malfunction.

Television

Television companies use satellites to transmit television programmes.

The advantages of using satellites rather than cables are:

- Satellites can cover the surface of the Earth regardless of political and geographical problems on the surface, making television available to all with a receiver.
- They handle a large bandwidth which, especially through digital signal compression, can contain many channels.

Most lighthouses have closed as navigators no longer have to consult maps to find hazards on the coast. GPS tells them exactly where they are, even in fog or the dark.

However, there are disadvantages:

● Satellite television does not offer broadband services such as those offered with a cable modem.
● Satellite is not two-way; you only receive a signal.

5 *Standards and communications*

Standards in hardware and software are the rules for helping to create them and the levels of performance they should achieve. There are standards in most things these days. The Foods Standards Agency, for instance, makes sure that the food we eat is 'up to standard' and obeys the rules for what goes into the food and how it is made. It is important that software follows the rules so that it will work on hardware. The manufacturers of computer hardware work to a set of standards, some laid down by law, such as those associated with electrical wiring, and some which everyone follows because it is accepted practice. A computer manufacturer would soon go out of business if its product had non-standard USB ports fitted.

The set of rules to be followed is known as a protocol. Protocols are usually defined by groups such as the **International Standards Organisation (ISO)**. Manufacturers will follow these protocols so that:

● software will work on hardware regardless of manufacturer
● technical help can be provided by third parties
● peripherals produced by one company will fit computers produced by another
● communication between devices becomes possible

For data to be transmitted across a network successfully it must be understood by the receiving station. The internet operates mainly with the set of protocols known as **Transmission Control Protocol/Internet Protocol (TCP/IP)**. Without these protocols, messages could not arrive at the selected destination, data would be broken into packets which would not be understood by other stations, mail would not work etc. Another well-known protocol is **Open System Interconnection (OSI)**. This is a model for how data should move round a network by dividing the task into seven **layers**, ranging from the basic physical way bits are transmitted to highly complex applications such as a database or email system. OSI enables manufacturers to target equipment or software to a particular layer without worrying about the entire transmission process, knowing that for the layer they are working on data will arrive from the layer below and be sent to the layer above.

You may have **uploaded** data to a website or downloaded data into your computer. This requires the **File Transport Protocol (FTP)**.

5.1 Impact

If a company did not adhere to the prevailing standards and protocols, it would go out of business. Customers would not be able to order goods online, and emails could not be sent or received. It would be impossible, or very difficult,

to send data to different parts of the company using different hardware or standards. The company would also have great difficulty buying hardware and software compatible with that already owned. The customers would lose confidence in the company and the company would find it hard to employ staff to operate the system.

Topic summary

Networks — LAN, WAN, VLAN and VPN; bus, ring and star topologies; client–server and peer-to-peer networks; internet and intranet.

Communicating data — bandwidth, types of communications media (cable, optical, wireless).

Network components — hub, switch, wireless access point, network interface card (NIC), wireless network interface card, router, gateway, repeater, bridge.

Servers — file server, mail server, print server, proxy server.

Communications applications — fax, email, bulletin boards, video-conferencing, internet relay chat (IRC), mobile phones, satellites.

Standards — protocols, usefulness for businesses.

Applications and limitations of ICT

1 Applications of ICT

1.1 Resources

All ICT systems rely on internal resources. These can broadly be defined as **human resources**, **technological resources** and **accommodation**.

The human resources are the people employed to operate the system. These may include managers, engineers, secretaries and computer operators. These human resources are valuable – to make the system efficient they need to be looked after. Ongoing training, good pay and conditions, a safe working environment and a feeling of being valued by the company are some of the things to be considered when managing the human resources. To help in this process, **human resource management systems** are available (see section 1.3).

The technological resources are the machines and software that make the system work. These resources will probably include computers, applications packages, input and output devices. Like the human resources, they should be valued and looked after. Regular updates to hardware and software, proper maintenance and reviews of the system should take place.

With such valuable human and technological resources, the accommodation in which they are housed needs to be suitable for maintaining the safety and wellbeing of humans and computers. The type of accommodation depends on the type of system. The aspects to be considered would be different for a hospital than for a garden centre, for instance, or for a nuclear power station or a corner shop.

1.2 Information

Information is important to companies. Details of customers, products, suppliers, plans, balance sheets, projections for the future, reports and analyses are not only vital to the wellbeing of a company, but much is also governed by Acts of Parliament (as shown in Topic 7). It is important that the information held by the company is reliable, accurate, up to date (where possible) and complete.

When information is exchanged, it must be exchanged accurately and in a timely manner. Information may be exchanged between a customer and a company, between departments in the company, between suppliers and the company etc. If the information is timely and accurate, the company will build a reputation for efficiency and should be successful.

To achieve reliable information it is necessary to use the following:
- input checks such as validation and verification
- security to ensure that data is not lost, stolen or infected by viruses
- regular updates
- appropriate measures to comply with the laws of the country regarding information use and storage
- encoding of information when being transmitted to ensure it cannot be read by an unauthorised person
- the correct level of detail – not too much and not too little

Table 11.1 shows some examples of inaccurate information and possible consequences.

Inaccurate information	Consequence
The number of hours a person works is recorded incorrectly.	The person receives the wrong pay.
A customer's address is stored with an incorrect postcode.	The goods never arrive.
A customer orders 10 tins of dog food, which is interpreted as 10 cartons of dog food (each holding 24 tins).	The customer gets 240 tins of dog food.
An electricity meter is read incorrectly. It should be read as 10001, but is recorded as 100001.	The customer gets a huge electricity bill.
A car number plate is read incorrectly.	The wrong person is asked to pay a fine for speeding.
A company orders 100 tonnes of sand from Birmingham.	Sand arrives from Birmingham, Alabama and costs a fortune in delivery charges.
J. Smith is recommended for a bonus.	Janet Smith instead of John Smith is delighted to receive the bonus.
Mr Brown dies.	Mrs Brown gets a letter addressed to 'Mr Brown deceased'.

Table 11.1 Some consequences of inaccurate information

1.3 Systems

Most systems involve some measure of ICT involvement these days, particularly those using telecommunications and computers. Some of these are explored below.

Telephone systems

Telephone systems offer a range of services, such as:

- **Answering services** — these are sometimes automated and can be remotely controlled. Unwanted calls can be screened, caller IDs let you know who is calling, voice mail can be used, messages can be forwarded.
- **Call-back** — you can dial 1471 to find out who called you and then call back if you want to. You can find out who called but did not leave a message. You can block this facility to avoid being traced.
- **Ring-back** — if the phone is engaged, it will automatically ring you when the number becomes free.
- **Call waiting** — while you are having a conversation, you can be alerted to another call waiting for your attention.
- **Automatic control of a system using phone keypad** — used to order cinema tickets, check bank/credit card accounts or to control household devices such as central heating remotely.

- **Ex-directory directory classification** — used if you do not want to appear in the telephone book.
- **Call barring** — this stops the phone being used for dialling premium rate numbers.
- **Personalised ring tones** — so you know if the call is for you or someone else in the home or office.
- **Conference calls** — this facility links a number of people into the call, sometimes using video phones, which is useful for teleworking (working from home) and in distance learning such as the Open University.

Call centres

A company can set up a call centre that can handle large volumes of phone calls. The operators usually sit in large rooms in front of a computer, and wear a headset consisting of microphone and earphones to leave their hands free to use the computer to look up information, make bookings and record customer details.

Supervisors can listen in to calls and intervene if necessary. Operators can also make outgoing calls to customers, often **cold calling** (ringing without a prior invitation), to sell something or gain information. Businesses using call centres include:

- utility companies (gas, electricity, water)
- mail-order catalogue firms
- computer hardware and software firms for customer support
- internet providers for customer support
- banks and building societies
- insurance companies

Many call centres are in countries far away from the central company. As labour is cheaper and working conditions less strict than in the home country, this makes economic sense.

Banking

Banks have used computers to clear cheques for many years. At the bottom of every bank cheque is the cheque number, the sort code and the bank account number of the account holder (using a special font and magnetic ink).

Once a cheque has been filled in, the magnetic ink characters can be read by a machine that uses **magnetic ink character recognition (MICR)**. This is an efficient way to transfer the essential information to the bank's computers without error. MICR is used because cheques are often folded or may become dirty and so other computer-read characters might not be read accurately.

Most banks use **automated teller machines (ATMs)** to allow customers to pay in or take out money, even when the banks are closed. ATMs are located in many public places, such as outside supermarkets, in garages and at motorway service areas.

Electronic funds transfer at point of sale (EFTPOS), **electronic funds transfer (EFT)** and **smart cards** are described in Topic 7.

Production control

By involving ICT in the production of goods, efficiency and productivity can increase and costs can go down. For example:

- ICT stock control can minimise the amount of storage and number of spares a company needs to keep in stock, and allow items to be found quickly when needed. Stock control is explained more fully overleaf.
- Robotic devices are more efficient than humans as they can work productively without getting tired, going on strike or needing pay and holidays. For example:
  - Fixed robots can be used for welding and other repetitive tasks.
  - Roving robots, such as automatically guided vehicles, can be used for fetching goods by following special tracks.
- ICT can analyse the production and model alternative approaches.

ICT has affected methods of production by introducing robotics and other systems in order to help production control and **process control**. Process control is the control of the process of production, whether this is the temperature of liquid in a vat, putting caps on bottles in a production line or programming robots to carry out tasks. This had an effect on:

- the speed of the process
- the cost of the process
- the safety of the workers
- the quality of the final product

This in turn has led to (in most cases) better health and safety for employees and safer working practices, but much skilled labour is no longer required and the number of people employed in manufacturing industries has gone down. However, more people are required to work with ICT.

Human resource management (HRM) systems

Human resource management (HRM) is the administration and management of the people who work for a company. With the merging of ICT systems and HRM, the possibilities for more complex analysis and management of the employees becomes apparent. HRM can use ICT to support recruitment, selection, hiring, job placement, performance appraisals, employee benefit analysis, training development, health, safety and security.

Specifically, organisations use ICT to assist in the following HRM tasks:

- Selection of staff from within the organisation and from outside.
- Evaluation of employees by tracking:
  - their personal history
  - personal data held about them
  - their skills and qualifications
  - their capabilities, perhaps as management material or as researchers
  - their previous experiences in the current organisation and elsewhere
  - their payroll records, which will include holidays taken, days off sick as well as pay received and contributions made

Some roving robots can report if they are not working properly and plug themselves into a power supply if their charge is dropping.

- Payroll processes:
  - gathers data on employee time and attendance
  - calculates deductions such as taxes and pension contributions
  - generates pay cheques and probably sends money directly to the employee's bank using EFT
  - issues tax returns
  - sends information to the accounts department for record-keeping purposes
- Time and labour management:
  - uses new technology to collect information about employees' attendance – 'clocking-in' and 'clocking-out' are not always easy to check in the modern world of flexible working, job-share, working from home etc.
  - evaluates and analyses employee time/work information
  - monitors the computers, checkouts etc. that the employees are using for relevant activity
- Benefits administration which tracks employee participation in:
  - private healthcare
  - insurance policies
  - pension plans
  - profit sharing
  - stock options

Stock control systems

Keeping track of stock is important to an organisation. Large amounts of stock mean expensive storage areas have to be found and managed. Stock may be perishable (food stuffs), subject to corrosion (metal objects) or may become obsolete (electronic goods). Large amounts of stock mean more expense, as money has to be spent buying, storing and using people to supervise the excess. Supermarkets avoid this situation by keeping most of their stock on the store's shelves. The stock control system allows them to run a 'just-in-time' system by anticipating how much stock will be sold in the next few days and replacing it just before it runs out. An efficient stock control system probably means an efficient and profitable business. Stock control systems:

- keep a record of the number of goods in stock
- keep a record of the goods sold
- help the management to plan purchases for the future
- monitor the sales
- undertake automatic reordering
- keep a track of purchase dates of products to make sure they are sold when fresh, i.e. do not exceed the 'sell by' date

Automatic reordering is when a stock control system is able to automatically trigger an order for goods (e.g. by sending an electronic message to the warehouse or supplier) when the stock in the shop reaches a level known as the **reorder level**. The stock control system also has information about the quantities to order based on seasonal and other factors. Christmas puddings sell well in December but badly in July. Sometimes a company uses an advertising campaign, perhaps with television adverts, for a particular product

and it will expect this product to sell better during the campaign. Hot weather increases sales of fans and suntan lotion, while cold weather sends people out for gloves and anti-freeze. Stock control systems assist managers in keeping customers satisfied and running an efficient business.

Computer-aided design and computer-aided manufacture (CAD/CAM)

The main features of a CAD/CAM package are:

- a computer-aided design process
- automatically calculating stresses and strains, checking electrical circuits etc.
- automatically working out costs
- linking directly to and controlling a process in a factory
- helping with the supply of materials
- scheduling jobs in the production process

Expert systems

An expert system consists of a database of knowledge gathered by experts known as the **knowledge base**. There is a set of rules (the **rule base**) built in to the system which has to be followed. By combining the rules and the knowledge and by asking questions via an interactive interface, the expert system can assist the non-expert to reach a solution to a problem. Most computers have a simple built-in expert system to help solve straightforward problems, such as the printer not working or failure to connect to a network. More complex systems are used in commerce, science and medicine. For instance, an expert system could be used in a hospital by doctors to help diagnose an illness. The system asks a number of questions based on the patient's symptoms. The doctor enters the answers into the system. The system then uses artificial intelligence (an **inference engine**) to combine the knowledge base with the rule base to reach a diagnosis of the patient's illness. This is particularly helpful if the hospital does not have human experts on hand to diagnose the problem, e.g. for very rare diseases where there are only a few experts in the world. It is also useful if the hospital does not have many doctors. In this case, the initial screening can be carried out by less qualified people, leaving the doctor to carry out the more demanding work.

Expert systems can be found in a number of areas:

- oil and mineral exploration
- medicine
- help-desk applications
- grammar checkers
- creating other expert systems

There are disadvantages to using expert systems. They are not always right and the user should use common sense and judgment when considering a solution offered by the system. The expert system can only produce a solution which is as good as the data entered by the user and the quality of the system. Very good systems can be expensive.

Applications of ICT

Analogue signals are continuously variable and are not discrete, whereas digital signals are formed of just two states, represented by 0s and 1s.

Digital television

When television was first broadcast to people's homes, it was in **analogue** format, which later developed to include colour, stereo sound and more lines of dots on the screen to make the picture clearer. However, there were limits to the range of services offered by the analogue system, and **digital** television networks were perceived to be the answer. Analogue television broadcasts are now being phased out in favour of digital ones.

This means that many people have to buy new television sets, but in the long run the choice of stations and quality of pictures and sound will be enhanced. Television companies will have to compete with a greater number of rival companies, and it will be possible to have channels devoted to minority subjects, such as shopping or niche sports.

Digital television uses state-of-the-art digital technology to transmit perfect pictures in a number of display formats, including high and standard definition television, in both conventional and wide-screen versions. Sound is of CD quality (no interference), with up to six channels of surround sound. In the standard definition mode, broadcasters are able to transmit up to six completely separate programmes simultaneously. As well as transmitting the programmes, it is possible to transmit subtitles for the hard of hearing or in different languages, and sound descriptions in silent parts of films for the visually impaired. When digital television is combined with cable, it is possible to have an interactive system where viewers have an impact on what they are viewing or how they view it. Some additional services offered by cable television are:

- access to email and internet services through the television set
- shopping using the remote control
- controlling which camera to view the action from when watching sporting events or reality television
- taking part in quizzes, gambling or game shows from home
- watching programmes on demand
- choosing happy or sad endings to dramas
- pausing the programme to resume watching it later

Computer-aided learning (CAL)

Computer-aided learning uses a computer to provide instructional information to a student, to pose questions and to react to the student's response. **Computer-based training** and **e-learning** are other terms used to describe the use of ICT to allow an individual to receive training without the physical presence of a human teacher. Table 11.2 lists the advantages and disadvantages.

Advantages of CAL	Disadvantages of CAL
It is often cheaper for the employer than hiring a teacher.	The trainee needs access to a computer.
Training can be done at any time suitable for the trainee.	The knowledge learned may be wrong.
Training can be done at home.	The trainee cannot check immediately with a teacher.
A trainee can study at his/her own pace and does not have to match the speeds of other members of a group.	The data used by the system may not be up to date or accurate.
Employers/teachers can monitor the trainee's progress.	There is no human contact, which can be lonely.
Sections can be repeated as often as necessary until they are understood.	
'Fast track' is possible for bright trainees or those who already have a good knowledge of the subject.	

Table 11.2 The advantages and disadvantages of CAL

Management information system (MIS)

A management information system (MIS) is a system of analysing data to provide understandable management-level information. A MIS converts data from internal and external sources into information which can be used for planning, directing or controlling a business. It can be used for making tactical and strategic decisions, analysing sales data and highlighting sales trends. Generally, it is an aid to making effective decisions.

2 Distributed databases

A distributed database is one in which the files are shared across the network. Because the database is distributed, the data must be synchronised regularly to ensure data consistency. There are a number of ways in which the distribution can take place. Three of them are described below.

2.1 Partitioned between sites

Each remote processor has data with which it is primarily concerned, such as its own customers or stock. Users on different sites, such as headquarters, can view what is held in the database, but do not physically hold copies. This method means that security is increased because the whole database is not held at the local site. Efficiency is improved because the local partition of the database only has to manipulate part of the data. Backing up the data is faster because each separate part is backed up by the remote site.

If part of the database was held in a country with less stringent data protection laws, that part of the data may be at risk. However, intercepting the data would be difficult since actual data stays at the site and only queries to produce reports are run over the network.

Horizontal partitioning occurs when one or more tables are split in such a way that certain rows or records are dealt with by one location and other rows by another location. For instance, all customers who have a postcode beginning with the letters GL could be dealt with by a company's Gloucester office, and all those whose postcode begins with WR by the Worcester office. Although the data would be split for most of the time, headquarters could have an overall view of the entire database.

In large databases, attributes (details) of the entities are often collected and stored but not used. This means that a number of columns in a table in a distributed database are moved around without ever changing. This results in slower searching. A solution would be to split a table using **vertical partitioning**. The parts of the table would be distributed to the areas where they were best needed and little used parts could stay with the main data at headquarters. An overall view could be created. Although on the rare occasion where unusual data was needed, the information would take longer to build up, this would be offset by the increase of speed in the analysis of any separate section of the database.

2.2 Duplicated at each site

Using this method, the database is uploaded each night and alterations made to include the local changes by merging the different versions. This means that more than one copy of the database exists at any one time. If the databases are held in sites in different time zones there might be problems with reconciling data at the end of working days that finish at different times. If any one version is destroyed, however, the others still exist and only the transactions made that day are lost from one site. Possibilities of interception of data exist, as a huge quantity of data is moved around between sites while merging the daily changes to the master copy of the database. The advantage of duplicating in this way is that local searches can be carried out quickly, but analysis of the data would be slower than with partitioning as there is so much data and each local copy is not globally up to date.

2.3 Central database with remote local indexes

Every database consists of tables and indexes. Indexes help to speed up the searching efficiency of a database by indicating where to find records which might be needed when queries are run. Some databases create running indexes as data is entered. Using this method, the central database does not hold any of the actual data but just a collection of indexes for the data held on remote sites. The FBI Laboratory's **Combined DNA Index System Program (CODIS)** consists of an index of DNA collected from convicted offenders and another index of DNA recovered at crime scenes. Each state participating in CODIS retains control of its own data but the FBI holds the indexes.

<table>
</table>

3 *Limitations of ICT*

3.1 Identity theft

Most people have received at some point a **phishing** email. Often it purports to have been sent by a bank at which you were not even aware you had an account. The email asks for personal details, using something like a 'restructuring of the system' as a reason. The purpose is to steal your identity. Once armed with your bank account details, your name and address, the phishers can apply for credit cards, buy goods and steal your money. Because it is easy to bank or shop online it can be easy for criminals to take advantage of us and our data if we are not vigilant. We must be as careful as we can with our data so that we do not become electronically cloned and to prevent someone else pretending to be us, opening bank accounts and running up debts in our name.

3.2 Personal data

As more and more data about us is held on computers, we need laws to govern that data and to try to prevent it falling into the wrong hands. The difficulties are that with data held electronically, it is easy to search (and steal) enormous quantities of data in seconds and, in the case of stealing, leave no trace. Unscrupulous people would like to know which famous people are HIV positive or have criminal convictions so that they can blackmail them or sell the revelations to the newspapers. Discriminatory groups want to know who has belonged to religion or a certain political party, who they phone or email and what they say. It is wonderful to have a mobile phone crammed full of telephone numbers of friends, copies of messages sent and received and pictures of our families. However, if the phone should fall into someone else's hands all that information is now theirs, with possible negative consequences.

3.3 Commerce and data

Commercial organisations want to know our habits: whether we are married, how much we earn, whether we are gamblers, whether we keep pets. All this information can be used to target us with advertising. Much of this is legitimate – and if we are vegetarians we would not want to receive lots of adverts for meaty products. However, we need to be constantly aware that our computers are now linked (potentially) to any other computer in the world (imagine several billion people having access to your private files). We need to have spyware, firewalls, off-line data, virus checkers etc. to prevent this happening. There is an old saying that whenever a lock is created, someone else will find the key, so we have to be constantly vigilant, always trying to keep one step ahead of the 'bad guys', and never becoming complacent with our security arrangements.

3.4 Human error

GIGO was mentioned in Topic 1 – if incorrect data is put into a computer system, inaccurate results will result. This is a limitation that everyone who uses computers should be aware of. It might lead to something trivial like receiving an incorrect bill because someone keyed in an incorrect order, or something much more serious such as being sent a parking fine after a user keyed in an incorrect car registration number. Just because computers are fast and reliable does not make them infallible.

3.5 Over-dependency on ICT

Computers are so useful that we rely heavily on them. Most of our addresses and phone numbers, email addresses, favourite sites on the internet etc. are stored on an ICT-based device. All our music and entertainment may be on a electronic player. We may have reached the stage where we cannot write without cutting and pasting from someone else's work found on the internet. If there was a sudden shortage of batteries or a breakdown in electrical supply, would we still be able to function? The danger of becoming over-dependent on technology is something that we should all be aware of. Finally, we should not become too trusting of ICT-based information in our lives. When we read something on the internet, for instance, we should reserve judgement until we have confirmed what we have read from other sources. We need to have alternatives, and never hand over our lives to computers completely.

3.6 Problems of disposal

As a consumer society we are continually upgrading our ICT equipment and throwing away the old. This disposal must be done responsibly or parts of our environment may be spoiled. Many of these devices contain potentially dangerous components, such as printed circuit boards, cables, wires, plastics containing flame retardants, mercury switches, displays (e.g. cathode ray tubes), batteries, data storage media, capacitors resistors.

3.7 Politics

All this sounds pessimistic, but by being vigilant, and electing a government that takes the threats seriously and will create laws to help protect us, the positive sides of ICT in our lives should be greater than the negatives. Topic 7 mentions several Acts of Parliament that have been set up to govern ICT and ICT-related issues.

Topic summary

Resources — human, technological, accommodation.

Information — reliable, accurate, up to date.

Systems — telephone, call centres, banking, production control, human resource management, stock control, computer-aided design and manufacture, expert systems, digital television, computer-aided learning, management information.

Distributed databases — partitioned, duplicated, remote local indexes.

Limitations of ICT — identity theft, personal data, commerce and data, human error, over-dependency on ICT, problems of disposal, politics.

1 Upgrading systems

1.1 Off-the-shelf software versus custom-written software

Many applications packages on sale have been written to enable people to carry out routine tasks such as word processing, creating databases and writing web pages. More specialist types of software include those for editing photographs, producing a school timetable or designing a new home. In fact, whenever there is a sufficient number people wishing to carry out a particular activity on the computer to make producing software commercially viable, someone will have written it. When a person or company has a need which is not met by software that is readily available (**off-the-shelf software**), programmers have to be employed to write **custom-written software**.

The person or group requiring the new software is known as the **client**. The client identifies the problem that needs solving and it is up to the firm recruited to write the new software system to understand the problem well enough to provide a working solution. The following is a list of steps which should be followed when producing a custom-written computer-based system:

- An initial meeting is held with the client to discuss the project.
- The needs of the client are identified and agreed.
- A design is created and agreed.
- Initial drafts of the program are produced.
- Test plans are created and the tests carried out.
- Prototyping of user interfaces involves the client.
- Data structures are created.
- Bugs are fixed and a beta version is written and tested by the client.
- The new system is installed for the client.
- Documentation is written.
- Training is given.

A custom-written solution can be expensive and time-consuming and there is no guarantee that a working solution can be produced. The UK government has, over the years, spent billions of pounds commissioning high-profile systems for the health service, the courts and the police, to mention just a few, which were later abandoned as not producing the desired solution. Software solutions in common use have been tried and tested and are quick and relatively cheap to buy. A one-off solution, however, has training implications for staff who are unfamiliar with the new system, and there is little support available.

There are problems associated with all software. The computers on which the software runs rapidly become obsolete. The firm that produced the software may stop trading or lose interest in supporting that particular program. Table 12.1 gives advantages and disadvantages of the different types of software.

Off-the-shelf software is already written and can be purchased in shops. Custom-written software has to be specially written for the client.

Testing carried out by the producers is known as white-box testing. Black-box testing is carried out by the client.

Alpha versions of programs are tested by the producers. Beta versions are tested by the client.

	Advantages	Disadvantages
Off-the-shelf	• The software should have most of the bugs removed as it has been in the public domain for some time. • There are existing users/help groups/online help. • The staff may already be familiar with the software so they will need the minimum of training. • There should be little or no decrease in the efficiency of operations immediately after installation. • It can be purchased and used almost at once. • It is relatively cheap to buy as it is already written and the costs are shared by a large customer base.	• It may require significant changes in working practices and so demand staff training. • It may not do exactly what is required and therefore involve further costs in adapting the software. • The software may have a larger memory footprint than a custom-written equivalent.
Custom-written	• The software will do exactly what is required. • There will be a smaller memory footprint than an off-the-shelf equivalent. • The software copyright will belong to the firm.	• The software will probably be more expensive than an off-the-shelf equivalent. • It may have more bugs than an off-the-shelf equivalent. • The staff will not be familiar with the software and need training. • Help may only be available from the original manufacturer. • There may be no user groups. • It will not be available immediately.

Table 12.1 Off-the-shelf software versus custom-written software

1.2 Making the decision

Before upgrading or installing software and hardware to any system, the current system must be reviewed to make sure that there will be benefits when the new system is working. Factors affecting that decision include:

- The expertise of the staff:
  - Will they be able to handle the new system?
  - Will they need training?
  - Will staff need to be hired or made redundant?
- The costs of the update:
  - Will the benefits of the new system outweigh the costs?
  - Will business be lost while the upgrades occur?

- The benefits of the new system:
  - Will the system be more efficient than the old one?
  - Will the system be competitive?
  - Will the costs of the new system be covered by the increase in business expected or the increased efficiency of the system?
- The method of installation:
  - Can the process be stopped to install the new system?
  - Will the new system will work once it is installed?
  - Are all parts of the new system fully developed?

2 *System installation*

There are four main methods of installing a new computer-based system:
- **Direct** (sometimes called immediate or 'big-bang')
  - The new system replaces the old system without any overlap.
  - This is best done at a weekend or some other quiet time such as a public holiday.
- **Pilot**
  - The new system is only used in one location first, so it is tested, before being fully installed.
- **Parallel**
  - The new system operates for a short period alongside the old system.
  - The old system stops after a certain time.
- **Phased**
  - Part of the new system replaces part of the old system while other tasks continue to use the old system.
  - The installation is spread over a period of time.

When considering the method to use to install a new system, it is necessary to decide which will be the best method to avoid disruption and to be practical. Some systems cannot be run in parallel, for instance a real-time system such as booking a holiday or ordering goods online. Table 12.2 gives advantages and disadvantages.

2.1 System review

New systems will need monitoring to check that they are functioning correctly – that they are meeting the objectives specified for the system. This monitoring is known as a **review**. Systems need to be reviewed regularly, perhaps as often as once a month. This will ensure that the system does not become obsolete. Problems can be reported as they occur. It is important that staff operating the system are asked for their opinion on how well the system is performing, as they are the ones who will spot the problems first. Following a review, maintenance may need to be carried out.

Installation method	Advantages	Disadvantages
Direct	• Duplication of work is minimised. • Time lost is minimised. • Possibly the cheapest method of installation.	• If the new system is faulty, business could be lost. • There is no possibility of comparing results from the original system. • Difficult to repair faults while continuing to run the business.
Pilot	• Results can be compared with the old system. • Bugs can be cleared from the system. • Training of staff can be modified in the light of experience gained. • Comments from customers can be taken note of before the system is installed in all locations.	• Extra work is necessary while the pilots are running, involving staff and costs. • Takes longer to install the new system.
Parallel	• If there are problems with the new system, the old system can be referred to. • The old system can be used as backup in case of error. • Training can take place for the rest of the workforce.	• Data will have to be recorded in both systems. • Staff may become stressed with the extra work. • The cost of parallel running is greater than other methods. • Increased accommodation must be arranged.
Phased	• The new system can be run in one location before being 'rolled out' to all locations, which allows bugs to be fixed. • Staff can be trained at the first location ready for the main changeover.	• Delays the start of full implementation. • Involves extra staff and costs. • This method is only possible with some systems.

Table 12.2 Advantages and disadvantages of the four installation methods

3 System maintenance

Maintenance is necessary as a computer-based system grows older. Bugs may be found in the system that were not originally identified, perhaps because appropriate tests were not devised or because an update in hardware in part of the system causes a crash with another part of the system. As time goes on, the needs of the customers change, new hardware and software becomes available and governments change laws on what can be stored, conditions in which staff work etc.

There are three main types of maintenance:

- **Adaptive maintenance**
  - if changes in working practices are identified in a review
  - if there is an increase in the number of customers
  - if new legislation is introduced by the government
- **Corrective maintenance**
  - if bugs and errors found in the system need correcting
- **Perfective maintenance**
  - if new technology becomes available which might allow the performance of the system to be improved
  - if a review indicates ways in which the system could be changed to enhance its performance

Topic summary

Upgrading systems — off-the-shelf software, custom-written software.

System installation — direct, pilot, parallel, phased.

System review — meeting the objectives specified for the system.

System maintenance — adaptive, corrective, perfective.

1   *The impact of external change*

In every organisation, some form of system life cycle takes place, from the original identification of a problem with the system to the review of that system, and finally the identification of a new problem. Often the problem in the system occurs because of **external** causes – events beyond the control of the organisation – so the organisation has to adapt its system to fit to the external changes. These changes can affect:

● an organisation
● individuals within the organisation
● the systems in use within the organisation

The changes may be brought about for a number of reasons. First, **economic changes**. In an economic recession, customers may not buy luxuries or visit restaurants. People stop spending on credit cards, and so overall purchasing goes down. This has an impact not only on any organisation that sells goods or services that could be considered non-essential to life, but also on the companies that lend money, such as banks, building societies and credit card companies. Changes may have to be made to the way the organisation works, so the system alters to adapt to the external change of less money being spent.

Currency changes may affect the cost or availability of raw materials that are used in a particular system. Paying for the raw materials for a system, for example beans to go in a tin, the metal to make the can or the energy to run the production line, can become more difficult if the monetary exchange rates change. This can make it more expensive, or sometimes cheaper, to buy the materials, meaning that the quantity of goods produced may have to change or that the methods of manufacture have to change to allow for the increased costs.

Changes in **legislation** might mean changing the system or working practices. For instance, laws relating to the storage of data, health and safety in working conditions, or discrimination in the workplace can have an impact on the system.

Advances in technology may mean a system has to change to keep up with other companies or because the old technology is no longer supported. For example, the user's software may not run on new machines, and printer cartridges and other consumables for aging hardware may no longer be produced. Sometimes an advance in technology makes it possible for an organisation to do something it had not considered before, perhaps because of the expense. For instance, a few years ago online shopping services were not offered by many companies. Now, almost all of them offer this service. Similarly, online banking, paperless utility bills sent by email and e-learning have changed the way that organisations operate. Changes in what is **fashionable** may be technological in origin, such as moving away from video recorders to DVD writers or hard disc recorders, or have less obvious causes, such as when particular colours, clothes or eating and drinking habits become fashionable.

External changes can have an effect on the staff at an organisation. As the system changes, so do their work practices. Changes in individual spending patterns by customers may lead an organisation to reduce its staff as it tries to make the system more efficient, or to take on staff as it tries to cope with

increased orders. The employees will have to retrain to cope with a new system, perhaps giving up skills acquired over the years and taking on new ones, which can be particularly hard as a person gets older.

Given the many external factors which can affect an organisation, the management must be vigilant to these changes in order to stay in business and be competitive.

2 *Managing change*

A number of factors should be considered when managing change, including:
- staff views of the changes
- staff capability
- systems and how they are implemented
- customer views
- equipment needed
- accommodation needed

Staff views should be taken into account. Without the workforce behind the organisation there might be resentment or even strikes, any of which may lead to a drop in efficiency and/or a loss of staff as employees 'vote with their feet' and leave for other organisations. It is important that the employees feel comfortable with the changes and aid the management to make a smooth transfer to the new system.

Staff capability must be considered. Some staff may have been with the firm for years. They may be highly skilled in some area of the old system, perhaps document filing or making machine parts, but under the new system these skills may no longer be required. Perhaps all filing will be electronic in a 'paperless' office, or the machine parts are to be made by robot. If these staff are not properly retrained, they may not be able to operate the new system. This could lead to resentment, unhappiness and loss of self-esteem, which in turn would lead to mistakes and inefficiency. Often, staff may have to be trained to do a different job within the organisation or to do the same job in a different way. Sometimes it will be necessary to make staff redundant if they are not able to fit into the new system.

System implementation needs to be carefully managed to ensure no loss of business while the change is taking place. Methods of implementation are discussed in Topic 12. Careful planning before this stage commences could mean the difference between success and failure. The method of changeover should be decided and when it will happen.

Customer views must not be forgotten and the customer base should be kept informed of the changes so that it is not lost to rival firms during the changeover. Customers are an important part of any business. Without the customer, there would be no need for the business. Customers should be consulted through user groups or questionnaires and kept informed of changes which may affect the way they purchase the goods or services of a company. Even something as simple as changing the way a customer is invoiced can be off-putting.

The **equipment** that is to form part of the new system must be carefully chosen to make sure that it does the job and will not become obsolete in a short time. If the organisation relies heavily on the equipment, e.g. in a production line, it must be thoroughly tested before total reliance is placed on it. Staff must be trained to operate it and hardware maintenance schedules put in place.

The **accommodation** must be suitable for the new system, providing room to hold it and the staff and, if necessary, room for future expansion. Health and safety laws must be considered, including those governing the use of computer equipment by staff. Conditions should be made comfortable for working, with air conditioning, proper lighting, seating, fire exits etc. The infrastructure of the area where the accommodation is to be built needs to be able to support the new business with, for example, broadband facilities, wide access roads and adequate utility supplies.

2.1 The role of the management

The process of changing to a new system is a difficult one, with many aspects to be considered. One of the most important of these factors is the people – employees and customers are crucial to an organisation's success. For any organisation to move to a new system efficiently there should be careful management of all aspects of the business, with special emphasis on keeping the workforce on-side.

When it comes to managing the changeover to a new system, it is important that employees and customers are considered, using:
- consultation
- participation
- communication

The management team oversees the changeover. These are senior people in an organisation who normally take the day-to-day decisions and issue orders to the workforce.

Consultation between the management team and the staff and customers is needed to ensure a successful changeover. A survey by the management team of the customers could be carried out to find out how the customers perceive the possible change, or what they expect from it. The staff should be consulted on points of expertise and given input into the change to a new system. If the new business is to be in a different area or town from the present site, perhaps the staff should be asked if they would be willing to work at the new site if they were offered travelling expenses or help with relocating. Any misgivings the staff may have about the new system need be listened to, so regular meetings will take place.

Participation will help to make the staff and customers feel more comfortable and confident about the change. Training opportunities need to be made available to both staff and customers. The transfer of the data from the old system to the new one needs to be managed without disruption or error and staff could participate in this process, giving them a stake in the new system before it is operational. Regular meetings with staff and the management team allow the staff to feel that they were participating in the change.

Communication is essential. Rumours and ill-informed gossip can cause resentment in a workforce ignorant of the facts. From the beginning, the employees need to be reassured by the management team that their jobs are secure, that their existing skills are not undervalued, or that training opportunities and job changes without loss of status or pay are possible. Management needs to explain the benefits of the new system to the staff to help them understand why it is necessary and what the consequences of not changing might be. Advertising campaigns or leaflets distributed to customers would explain the advantages of the new system. If the old system was electronic, customers might be informed on websites or by email. Timetables of planned changes and target dates for stages of the change should be well publicised and known to everyone in the organisation.

3 Ethics and professional bodies

Working and using ICT is covered by many Acts of Parliament. It is also useful for the individuals who work with ICT to have their own standards and codes of conduct. To help with this, professional bodies exist and ICT personnel can become members. Two of these organisations are the **British Computer Society (BCS),** which publishes a code of conduct, and the **Association for Computing Machinery (ACM)**, which has a code of ethics and professional conduct.

3.1 The purpose and activities of the BCS

The objectives of the BCS are to promote the study and practice of computing and to advance knowledge of and education in IT for the benefit of the public. It also awards qualifications such as Chartered Engineer. According to the BCS website, it 'enables individuals, organisations and society to realise the potential of and maximise the benefits from IT'.

The BCS:
- sets and maintains professional standards for its members
- produces a code of conduct which states, among other things, that the IT professional should:
  - have regard for the public health, safety and environment
  - have regard to the legitimate rights of third parties
  - have knowledge and understanding of relevant legislation
  - conduct their professional activities without discrimination against clients or colleagues
  - carry out work or study with due care and diligence
  - uphold the reputation and good standing of the BCS
  - seek to upgrade their professional knowledge and skill
  - observe the BCS Code of Good Practice
- produces a code of good practice which states, among other things, that the IT professional should:
  - maintain technical competence
  - adhere to regulations
  - act professionally as a specialist
  - use appropriate methods and tools
  - manage his/her workload efficiently

- participate maturely
- respect the interests of customers
- promote good practices within the organisation
- represent the profession to the public
- advises the government on ICT-related legislation
- initiates debates on ICT subjects

3.2 Code of ethics and professional conduct for the ACM

It is incumbent on all ACM members to:
- contribute to society and human wellbeing
- avoid harm to others
- be honest and trustworthy
- be fair and take action not to discriminate
- honour property rights including copyrights and patents
- give proper credit for intellectual property
- respect the privacy of others
- honour confidentiality

As computing professionals, every ACM member is also expected to:
- strive to achieve the highest quality, effectiveness and dignity in both the process and products of professional work
- acquire and maintain professional competence
- know and respect existing laws pertaining to professional work
- accept and provide appropriate professional review
- give comprehensive and thorough evaluations of computer systems and their impacts, including analysis of possible risks
- honour contracts, agreements and assigned responsibilities
- improve public understanding of computing and its consequences
- access computing and communication resources only when authorised to do so

3.3 The advantages and disadvantages of belonging to a professional body

Membership of a professional body is a sign to everyone, particularly employers, colleagues and clients, that the member's qualities are recognised by his/her peers. Professional recognition is becoming increasingly important as getting jobs becomes more competitive. It helps to create confidence which, in turn, creates better business relationships. It shows that the member is successful in his/her career and has high levels of knowledge and expertise in the field of ICT. Members are also connected to a network of other similarly qualified individuals and able to attend seminars, read newsletters, keep up to date with new legislation etc. There are also disadvantages. Professional bodies may use their power to restrict competition, so called 'closed shop' activities. They may also become self-serving and lose sight of the client.

4   *Advances in ICT*

ICT is constantly evolving and changing the way we do things, the way we communicate and even the words we use. DVD, HD, mobile, television, MP3, Xbox, ATM and other terms are part of our everyday language. Not only our language, but our ideas about what we are able to do with our computers, mobile phones and other electronic devices, would be incomprehensible to our great-grandparents. Technology is evolving at an increasing rate and costing less. However, we expect to spend more of our income on these 'non-essentials', and the percentage of our income spent on food has dropped in 70 years from around 25% to 5%. Try to think how you would manage in the event of a power cut and a global shortage of batteries to power devices to understand how much we rely on our electronic gadgets.

Technology moves so quickly – the speed at which processors work, the increasing amount that can be stored in a decreasing space, the increasing sophistication of the inputs and outputs and the advances in computer programming – that as we think of ICT in our lives we have to think of what could be possible tomorrow as well as what is possible today.

It is difficult to think of any area of life that does not involve ICT. Some of these advances can be considered as advantages, and some as disadvantages.

The characteristics of an ICT system can lead to abuse of ICT in society. These characteristics include:

- fast processing of repetitive tasks
- a very large storage capability
- the ability to search quickly for data or combinations of data
- the ability to combine data in many different ways
- presentation of information in various ways at the touch of a button
- improved accessibility to information and services

Various Acts of Parliament try to limit the abuse that can flow from the application of ICT. Improved security of data is important to prevent our lives becoming prey to cold callers, our identity being stolen and our bank accounts raided.

Great benefits can come from ICT developments (see Table 13.1), but it up to all of us to see that we do not become dependent on ICT and that we are always in control.

Area of advance in ICT	Advantages	Disadvantages
Treating injuries or disease	• Huge progress with artificial body parts as well as the unravelling of DNA and the possibility of designer drugs	• Developments in curing or preventing disease may have knock-on effects, such as the resistance of some kinds of bacteria to penicillin. These developments need to be carefully monitored.
Leisure activities	• Virtual reality games which give us exercise in our living rooms • Orienteering using GPS systems • Online booking for sporting events	• We have become increasingly remote from each other, retreating into a virtual world of chat rooms, headphones, mobile phones for texting and talking, and virtual reality games instead of real ones.
The environment	• Monitoring carbon monoxide emissions from central heating systems potentially saves lives • Checking exhaust emissions from motor vehicles • Air-conditioners	• Large quantities of old hardware need disposal and cannot be put into landfill because of dangerous elements used • A lot of energy is used to run all the machines and keep them on stand-by
The home	• Efficient central heating systems controlled by computer • Other household gadgets • Home banking • Home shopping • Helping older people and disabled people stay in their own home	• Reliance on ICT • Too many gadgets • Not enough exercise
Education	• Learning at home or distance learning including CAL • ICT used in education (see Topic 7) • Online research	• Loss of human interaction • Too much reliance on possibly inaccurate information gained from the World Wide Web
Freedom of speech	• Every country in the world has mobile phones, internet access etc. It is possible for any voice to be heard from anywhere and any point of view to be put across easily to millions	• Very difficult to keep things secret • An un-policed internet means that extreme views of hatred and intolerance can be transmitted to millions and can influence impressionable users
Freedom of movement	• Travel all over the world is safer with communications so easy • GPS makes finding your way around straightforward • Tracking devices can record your position anywhere so you can never be lost	• The increasing use of CCTV cameras, mobiles which can track our movements and possibly compulsory ID cards may impact on our liberty and create a 'Big Brother' state. • Our shopping habits and where-abouts are recorded as we use our credit and debit cards

Table 13.1 Advances in ICT

Topic summary

The impact of external change — economic change, legislative changes, advances in technology.

Managing change — staff views, staff capability, system implementation, customer views, equipment, accommodation.

The role of management — consultation, participation, communication.

Ethics and professional bodies — British Computer Society, Association for Computing Machinery, codes of practice.

Advances in ICT — treating injuries or disease, leisure activities